Understanding
BAPTIST POLITY

Lee H. McCoy

Convention Press

NASHVILLE   TENNESSEE

Code Number: Church Study Course
This book is number 1604 in category 16, section
for Adults and Young People

Library of Congress catalog card number: 64-10973
Printed in the United States of America
7.5 AT 63 R.R.D.

DEDICATED TO J. M. PRICE

*who first made the author aware
of the importance of understanding
Baptist polity*

About the Author

LEE H. McCOY was born in Guthrie, Oklahoma, February 14, 1915. He was educated in the public schools of Oklahoma and did his undergraduate work at Oklahoma Baptist University, where he received the B.S. degree. During his student days, he served as local and as state BSU president. After working for a short time in the business world, he felt called of God to the ministry of religious education. In the fall of 1940, he entered Southwestern Baptist Theological Seminary, from which he received both the M.R.E. and D.R.E. degrees.

He has served as minister of education in First Baptist Church, Charlottesville, Virginia; First Baptist Church, Shawnee, Oklahoma; Olivet Baptist Church, Oklahoma City, Oklahoma; the First Baptist Church, Abilene, Texas. He also served part time in the Cornell and Ridglea Baptist churches in Fort Worth, Texas. His ministry in Charlottesville was interrupted by twenty-seven months service as a line officer in the United States Navy.

Since 1955, Dr. McCoy has taught in the School of Religious Education at Southwestern Baptist Theological Seminary, where he is professor of church administration. He is a frequent contributor to Baptist periodicals.

He was married in 1938 to Virginia Ann Cook, of Oklahoma. They have one daughter, Nancy Ann McCoy Enas, who lives in Fort Worth, Texas.

Contents

Church Study Course

THE CHURCH STUDY COURSE began October 1, 1959. It is a merger of three courses previously promoted by the Sunday School Board—the Sunday School Training Course, the Graded Training Union Study Course, and the Church Music Training Course. On October 1, 1961, the Women's Missionary Union principles and methods studies were added.

The course is fully graded. The system of awards provides a series of five diplomas of twenty books each for Adults or Young People, two diplomas of five books each for Intermediates, and two diplomas of five books each for Juniors. Book awards earned previously in the Sunday School Training Course, the Graded Training Union Study Course, and the Church Music Training Course may be transferred to the new course.

The course is comprehensive, with books grouped into twenty categories. The purpose of the course is to help Christians to grow in knowledge and conviction, to help them to grow toward maturity in Christian character and competence for service, to encourage them to participate worthily as workers in their churches, and to develop leaders for all phases of church life and work.

The Church Study Course is promoted by the Baptist Sunday School Board, 127 Ninth Avenue, North, Nashville, Tennessee, through its Sunday School, Training Union, Church Music, and Church Administration departments; and the Woman's Missionary Union, 600 North Twentieth Street, Birmingham, Alabama; and by the respective departments in the states affiliated with the Southern Baptist Convention. A description of the course and the system of awards may be found in the leaflet "Trained Workmen," which may be obtained without charge from any one of the departments named.

A record of all awards earned should be maintained in each church. A person should be designated by the church to keep the files. Forms for such records may be ordered from any Baptist Book Store.

Requirements for Credit in Class
or Home Study

IF CREDIT is desired for the study of this book in a class or by home study, the following requirements must be met:

I. IN CLASSWORK

1. The class must meet a minimum of seven and one-half clock hours. The required time does not include assembly periods. Ten class periods of forty-five minutes each are recommended. (If laboratory or clinical work is desired in specialized or technical courses, this requirement may be met by six clock hours of classwork and three clock hours of supervised laboratory or clinical work.)

2. A class member who attends all class sessions and completes the reading of the book within a week following the last class session will not be required to do any written work for credit.

3. A class member who is absent from one or more sessions must answer the questions (pp. 117-18) on all chapters he misses. In such a case, he must turn in his paper within a week, and he must certify that he has read the book.

4. The teacher should request an award for himself. A person who teaches a book in the section for Intermediates or Juniors (any category) or conducts an approved unit of instruction for Nursery, Beginner, or Primary children will be granted an award in category 11, Special Studies, which will count as an elective on his own diploma. He should specify in his request the name of the book taught, or the unit conducted for Nursery, Beginner, or Primary children.

5. The teacher should complete the "Request for Book Awards—Class Study" (Form 150) and forward it within two weeks after the completion of the class to the Church Study Course Awards Office, 127 Ninth Avenue, North, Nashville, Tennessee 37203.

II. In Home Study

1. A person who does not attend any class session may receive credit by answering all questions for written work as indicated in the book (pp. 117-18). When a person turns in his paper on home study, he must certify that he has read the book.

2. Students may find profit in studying the text together, but individual papers are required. Carbon copies or duplicates in any form cannot be accepted.

3. Home study work papers may be graded by the pastor or a person designated by him, or they may be sent to the Church Study Course Awards Office for grading. The form entitled "Request for Book Awards—Home Study" (Form 151) must be used in requesting awards. It should be mailed to the Church Study Course Awards Office, 127 Ninth Avenue, North, Nashville, Tennessee 37203.

III. Credit for This Book

This book is number 1604 in category 16, section for Adults and Young People.

Understanding Baptist Polity

CHAPTER 1

1

The Relationship of Church Polity and Church Government

SOUTHERN BAPTISTS are facing many challenges. Their polity and its application in the government of churches, associations, and conventions present several especially pertinent challenges. Questions are being raised about their governmental practices. Traditional ways of doing things are undergoing careful scrutiny in order to determine their validity. Studies are being made of organizational structures to discover and eliminate weaknesses. The need for greater efficiency and economy of operation is considered so important that many believe it warrants the delegation of powers to responsible officials.

This evaluation of Southern Baptists' work and attempts to analyze their weaknesses and their strengths have raised a number of significant questions. Must time-honored principles of polity be sacrificed? Has pure democracy become impractical in the large and complex operations of mid-twentieth-century churches? Should church polity be fluid rather than fixed? Should it be changed to meet the needs and problems of a changing environment? What should be the basis for determining polity?

I. THE RELATION OF POLITY AND GOVERNMENT

How a church is governed is largely determined by its polity. Polity is the theory and form of the governmental system. It signifies the principles which operate when a church either governs itself or is governed by others.

3

Polity and government are closely akin in meaning and are inseparably related. Polity denotes the seat of authority; government exercises the authority. Polity denotes the constitution or structure of government; government provides the structure. Polity denotes the method of government; government rules according to the method. Polity denotes the basis of membership; government regulates the membership. Polity denotes the way of doing; government sees that it is done. Polity denotes the type of government; government maintains the type of polity.

Good government in a church, then, is dependent upon a clearly defined polity. The starting point is the polity; government follows and implements the application and practice of this polity.

Although this book defines Baptist polity, many of the references will be to "government," the working out or implementation of polity, as it relates to the local church.

II. THE NEED FOR GOVERNMENT IN A CHURCH

Government is needed whenever two or more persons are associated together. Even a family must have rules to govern the activities of its members. These rules are worked out in the main by the father and the mother. Government is also necessary in the school, in the shop, or, in short, anywhere a group of people live or work together.

Whenever people engage in group activity of any kind, guidance must be given to their activity; that is, there must be government. The best type of government is designed according to what is best for the group and with rules which the group understands and follows willingly.

A good citizen governs himself according to the rules of the group to which he belongs. If any member of the group is unwilling to abide by them, there must be authority to enforce the rules. The absence of such authority makes government ineffective.

What about a church? Does it also need some form of government? There are those who answer no. They believe that government is not needed in a church and that the members can get along better without it. But experience has taught otherwise. The absence of government in a church, as in any other group, inevitably results in confusion and often in chaos.

The lack of government in a church could be a temptation to a few members to gain authority for themselves, with each one seeking to further his own personal interests. Conflicts and injustices would prevail. Ultimately, the strong would dominate and subjugate the weak. Factions would form. Progress in achieving the main purposes of the church would come to a standstill.

Not long after Christ commissioned his church and returned to the Father, it became evident that church government was needed. The members attempted to have all things in common, but soon there was complaining and conflict because of the alleged unfair treatment of the Greek-speaking widows. At the suggestion of the apostles, a simple type government was established, and seven men were elected to office. Order and harmony were restored. It is significant that soon afterward "the word of God increased; and the number of the disciples multiplied in Jerusalem greatly" (Acts 6:7).

III. The Purpose of Government in a Church

Many believe that the most important task of the government of the United States is "insuring domestic tranquility." The government of a church serves essentially the same purpose. It provides the framework within which members work together to know and do the will of Christ in a peaceful, orderly, and efficient manner. Its function is to maintain harmony and prevent discord in all relationships.

Government in a church enables members to do collectively what they could not do individually. For example, a Christian alone cannot take the gospel to all the world; but in joining heart and hand and money with others in the co-operative work of his church and denomination, he can carry out Christ's commission. Through the operation of government in his church, decisions are made and actions are taken that make this possible.

Baptists in particular have another purpose for good government in their churches. It serves to enlarge the liberties and opportunities of each individual. The belief in soul competency and individual freedom is one of the principal reasons why Baptists insist on the congregational type of polity in their churches.

IV. THE FUNDAMENTAL CHARACTER OF CHURCH POLITY

The polity of a church not only determines the manner in which the church is governed; it also affects its doctrine. History has proved that departure from the New Testament principles of polity results in departure from New Testament doctrine. The maintenance of polity is therefore important to the maintenance of beliefs. This makes polity very important in the life and work of a church.

Departure from New Testament polity is usually in the direction of greater centralization of authority. Often it is caused by an effort to achieve greater efficiency. Or it may be sought to satisfy a hunger for power and prestige by ambitious men. Whatever the motive, the consequences are usually the same: there is the compromise of New Testament teaching and the ultimate loss of spiritual power.

In the establishment of churches, through the centuries,

varied types of polity have developed. Comprehension of these several types is essential to an understanding of how Southern Baptists govern themselves.

V. The General Types of Church Polity

Although there are variations, the types of polity in existence today can be classified into four general categories: episcopal, monarchial, presbyterian, and congregational. A fifth type, which does not exist in this country, is Erastian. In Erastian polity, the church is linked to the state and advocates civil authority as supreme in church matters. The Church of England and the Lutheran Church in Germany are examples of this type.

1. *Episcopal*

The word "episcopal" comes from the Greek word which means overseer or bishop. Episcopal polity denotes the form of government in which bishops oversee the affairs of churches. Churches are grouped together in territorial divisions (episcopates) with a bishop having authority over each. These bishops, in turn, comprise a ruling body with jurisdiction over the subdivisions and churches in their territories. In the churches, a vestry, or board of officials, manages the temporal affairs.

The distinction between laity and clergy is strongly emphasized in true episcopal polity. While in recent years lay representation has increased, authority for the most part is entrusted to the clergy, among whom there is a system of gradation and rank.

Actually, episcopal polity follows the pattern of an oligarchy in which the ruling powers belong to a few. Authority is centralized at the top. In its higher form, the bishops are considered to be in direct line as successors of the apostles, and any practices or regulations not ordained by them are considered to be invalid.

No church or denomination in the United States practices episcopal polity in its pure form. The Protestant Episcopal Church and the Methodist Church practice this type in varying degrees and with certain modifications. For example, the Episcopal Church has a High-Church and a Low-Church party. The High-Church party stresses the episcopacy (rule of the bishops) while the Low-Church party believes that while episcopacy may be best, it is not altogether necessary. In either case, however, this alignment is usually determined more by the allegiance of the rector (pastor) than by the choice of the members.

The General Convention is composed of two houses: the House of Bishops (all bishops in the country) and the House of Clerical and Lay Deputies. The latter group is composed of an equal number (not more than four) of clerical and lay delegates from each diocese and one clerical and one lay nonvoting delegate from each missionary jurisdiction. In the church, a vestry of laymen not only manage the temporal affairs but also choose the rector in case of a vacancy, usually after consulting with the bishop.

Lay representation in the two conventions is more characteristic of presbyterian polity than episcopal.

In the structure of Episcopal Church polity, sufficient authority resides in the House of Bishops and in the descending ranks of the clergy to control the governmental processes of the Church.

In the Methodist Church, the distinction between laity and clergy is not as strongly emphasized as in the Episcopal Church, and the laity shares more extensively in the government. For example, the highest legislative and judicial body is the General Conference, which is made up of delegates from the Annual Conferences of the several territories. Half of the delegates in the General Conference are laymen. In the Annual Conferences, each pastoral charge has a lay delegate, along with all the ministers in the territory. There are, however, well-defined areas of authority in which lay delegates may not vote or participate. Questions of ordination, doctrine, or discipline are decided by the ministerial delegates.

A Methodist bishop is an official of first rank. He determines the number and boundaries of the districts within his territory and appoints a superintendent over each district. The superintendents in turn administer the discipline in their districts and have charge of the local ministers.

Methodist polity is modified episcopal. The division of the church into territories with a bishop in charge of each, the gradation of rank and office within the clergy, and the more extensive entrustment of authority in the ministers are all principles of episcopal polity.

2. Monarchial

Monarchial polity evolved out of episcopal polity. In fact, it is still classified by many writers as episcopal because authority is centered in the office of bishop. One of the basic distinctions is the elevation of one bishop above and over the other bishops. Monarchial polity is a self-perpetuating autocracy with a hierarchial structure. In fact, Episcopalianism—the doctrine that the authority to govern a church rests in a body of bishops and not in any one individual—was rejected by the Vatican Council of the Roman Catholic Church in 1870. Papal polity is the more appropriate designation when applied to the Roman Church. Monarchial is a more descriptive name for the polity practiced in any religious body where authority is centered in one supreme head, whether by constitution or usurpation.

The essence of monarchial polity is dictatorship. In papal polity, authority is centered in the Pope, who is the supreme and infallible head. Governing powers are channeled downward from him through a hierarchal structure of bishops and priests of descending ranks. The laity is excluded from all governmental authority, even in the management of temporal affairs. It has neither voice nor vote. Title and control of all properties belong only to the hierarchy.

In the Roman Catholic Church it is accepted that the Holy Spirit speaks to the Pope, the Pope to the bishops, the bishops to the priests, and the priests to the people. It is the duty of the people to accept and obey their edicts without question.

In monarchial polity, all governing power belongs to the clergy, none to the laity. Even in the local churches the priests are separated from the lay members and elevated above them. Pronouncements concerning doctrines, laws, and regulations of worship are to be accepted by the people as authoritative and final. The priests possess governmental powers and rule independently of the people.

3. *Presbyterian*

In presbyterian polity, authority is vested in presbyters, or elders, the latter being the more popular designation. In true Presbyterianism, the church is controlled by elders of equal rank, over whom there is no higher authority. This type of polity is sometimes referred to as representative or connectional polity. It is representative in that the elders represent the members who elect them. It is connectional in that there is an organic connection in the systematically arranged levels of government.

Since the Presbyterian Church is the best known of those that practice this type of polity, the discussion will be more directly concerned with the way it is practiced in that denomination. The Reformed churches, some Lutheran, and others employ this same general type of polity with certain variations.

Each Presbyterian church has a plurality of elders. One of these is a teaching elder (pastor); the others are elders (laymen) who govern. Each church also has deacons who look after temporal affairs. The distinction between the three—pastor, elders, and deacons—is carefully recognized. The pastor is not a member of the church, but of the presbytery of which the church is a part. The elders meet in the session, which is the governing body of the church. The pastor presides at this meeting.

The church in presbyterian polity, however, is considered a unit or a whole. As such, authority needs to be centralized. To achieve this, the individual churches are grouped in presbyteries. These are composed of all ministers within a certain district and one or two elders from each congregation. Presbyteries within a given area are grouped together to constitute synods. The highest court is the General Assembly, composed of all synods. Both the synods and the General Assembly are made up of the constituent members of the presbyteries.

Some of the larger synods are composed of elected representatives from the presbyteries; in others, all members of the presbyteries may attend. In the General Assembly, each presbytery is given a quota according to its size. Thus, in the polity of the church, there is a gradation of courts—the session, the presbytery, and synod, and the General Assembly.

In presbyterian polity, the General Assembly ultimately makes the major decisions. It determines doctrine and discipline. It may also set aside decisions, acts, or appointments made on lower levels. Appeals are made upward through the presbyteries and synods to the General Assembly. Authority flows downward from the General

Assembly through the synods and the presbyteries to the sessions in the churches and from the sessions to the congregations as a whole.

Presbyterian polity, then, is only semidemocratic for the people govern themselves only indirectly. They have the authority at the point of electing those who are to serve as elders, but once elected, the powers of government are delegated to them.

Presbyterian polity differs from episcopal polity in that there are no ranks or orders in the clergy. Rather, it is considered essential to maintain the equality of all ministers. Laymen (elders) who are elected to the various governing bodies also have equal authority with the ministers. In fact, laymen elected to a higher governing body actually exercise more authority than ministers in a lower governing body. Members in the churches also have more authority than those under episcopal polity, since they choose the officeholders and also help decide other matters related to the government in the congregation.

4. Congregational

The autonomy or self-government of the individual church is the chief characteristic of congregational polity. In this type of polity, the members of churches actually govern themselves. Final decisions in all matters rest with the vote of the whole congregation, not with a small governing group. Sometimes it is called independent polity because each church is completely independent of every other church and of every denominational body.

The very name "congregational" signifies the prominence of the congregation. No ascending denominational superstructure exists. Churches may associate for fellowship, doctrinal studies, and co-operation in missionary and denominational efforts. But in these assemblies there is no ecclesiastical union or governmental tie.

In congregational polity, each church is considered to be sovereign within the limits of its congregation. There must be no interference or exercise of authority from without or beyond the local body. No denominational body can either overrule the decision of a church or dictate to it. Within the church all members have equal rights and privileges. The pastor is regarded as the church's spiritual leader, but in matters of government, he has no more authority or right to voice his convictions than any other member. Decisions and courses of action are determined by vote after opportunity for free and full discussion has been given in the assembled congregation.

In congregational polity, each church is free to determine its doctrines, organizational structure, leaders, and activities. All officeholders, including the pastor, are elected by the church and are responsible to the church. Their responsibilities and the extent of their authority are defined by the church. Their decisions and actions are subject to the approval of the church. Their tenure of office is subject to the will of the church.

Baptists are the chief exponents of the congregational type of church polity. The Congregationalists, the Adventists, and the Disciples of Christ are other denominations that practice the same general type. So pronounced is the principle of autonomy of the individual church in their polity that they insist that there is no such organization as the church universal.

No other polity and government exists exactly like that of Southern Baptists. Although other denominations have similarities, when the whole of Southern Baptist polity and government is studied—in churches, associations, state conventions, and in the Southern Baptist Convention, and in the agencies of both the state and general conventions— it will be discovered that Southern Baptist polity and government are distinctive.

CHAPTER 2

2

New Testament Principles of Polity

"ALL SCRIPTURE is given by inspiration of God, and is profitable for doctrine, for reproof, for correction, for instruction in righteousness: that the man of God may be perfect, thoroughly furnished unto all good works" (2 Tim. 3: 16–17). The Scriptures are altogether adequate for a church both to determine and to judge its polity.

Although the Bible does not set forth explicit, detailed statements of church polity, God, in his wisdom, provided in the New Testament basic principles which are sufficient and authoritative in determining it. It is important that these principles be known, understood, and practiced by those who would remain true to Christ in the government of his church.

I. GOD, THE SOVEREIGN RULER OVER ALL MANKIND

God is revealed to men in the Scriptures as Father, Son, and Holy Spirit. While there is no division of nature, essence, or being, each has personal and unique attributes.

The sovereignty of God is the first and central doctrine of a church. Around it all other doctrines revolve. God reigns as the supreme and absolute ruler of the universe. As creator, sustainer, redeemer, and judge, he is sovereign over all the affairs of mankind. Paul proclaimed this great truth when he wrote, "For of him, and through him, and to him, are all things: to whom be glory for ever" (Rom. 11:36).

God is righteous in the exercise of his sovereignty. He accepts no compromise with sin and evil. Yet he does not force man to submit to his authority. He leaves him free to accept or reject, to obey or disobey. This does not mean that man may free himself from the demands of the sovereignty of God. He never ceases to be under God's divine authority. He will have to account to him for his behaviour. Christians and non-Christians alike are responsible to him for all they are, have, say, or do.

Although God is the sovereign ruler of the universe, he is the Heavenly Father who cares for his children. He exercises his sovereign powers in love and mercy. He draws near to his church in loving-kindness and tender mercy. Ideally, knowledge of his holy presence causes members of a church to submit themselves humbly to him as they seek to know and do his will. They recognize his majesty and power and his supreme authority in the government of a church. They think of the church first as a theocracy and then as a democracy. They determine their polity and government in the consciousness of God's higher authority over all things pertaining to the church.

II. CHRIST, THE HEAD AND DIVINE TEACHER OF THE CHURCH

God, in the person of Christ the Son, founded the church and maintains a vital connection with it. Christ is the head; the church is his body. As founder and head, he has all authority in all things pertaining to its life and work. God "hath put all things under his feet, and gave him to be the head over all things to the church, which is his body, the fulness of him that filleth all in all" (Eph. 1: 22–23).

Jesus is Son of man as well as Son of God. In his humanity he experienced what is in man and was tempted in all points like other men. This qualifies him in a peculiar way to exercise his authority as head of the church. God "hath given him authority to execute judgment also, because he is the Son of man" (John 5:27). A church is to seek to know what Jesus said and did concerning his church and then to conform to his ideal for the church.

In addition to reigning as head of the church, Christ is the divine teacher. His teachings are perfect. The measure to which a church departs from these teachings is the measure to which it rejects Christ as head of the church. The true New Testament church will consider it a duty and a privilege to follow the decisions already made for it by the divine teacher.

III. The Holy Spirit, Guide and Source of Power

Christ rules over his church through the Holy Spirit. He told his disciples: "When he, the Spirit of truth, is come, he will guide you into all truth: for he shall not speak of himself; but whatsoever he shall hear, that shall he speak: and he will shew you things to come. He shall glorify me: for he shall receive of mine, and shall shew it unto you" (John 16:13–14).

The Holy Spirit not only guides, he also empowers the church in its witness and work. He gives the power necessary for the implementation of the decisions he guides the church to make. New Testament church polity acknowledges the necessity of the Holy Spirit as the ever-present guide and source of all spiritual power. If he is ignored or rejected in the governmental affairs of a church, these affairs will have little spiritual significance.

A true New Testament church will acknowledge the Holy Spirit as the authoritative influence of Christ. It will seek his guidance in decision-making. It will seek the blessing of his power in its work. As a result, it will be able to govern its affairs in such a manner as to accomplish its world-encompassing task.

IV. The Bible, the Supreme Authority of the Church

Obedience to Christ demands that his church be governed according to the teachings in his Word. In it, the church is to find its final authority in matters of faith and practice.

A careful study of the New Testament reveals what Christ taught personally and through the Holy Spirit concerning his church. Since these teachings are of Christ, they are authoritative for churches of all times. Both the form and the practices of church government should always be in harmony with, and never contradictory to, what is preserved for the churches in his Word.

Some do not make the Bible the chief authority in determining their polity. They believe that church polity should be developed through expediency. Often such polity contradicts the principles found in the Scriptures. Baptists do not believe that the Holy Spirit leads in such contradictions. Christ sent the Holy Spirit to be present in the church to illuminate the Word of God, not to change it.

Methodists have developed their *Discipline*, which is the rule of the church. Presbyterians have their *Book of Church Order*. Others have similar books and creedal statements. Baptists reject everything but the Bible as their authority in church government. For them the Bible contains all that is needed to determine and to judge polity and governmental practices. They cling tenaciously to this principle because of their belief in the unerring nature of God's holy Word.

V. Each Individual, Competent and Free Under God

The New Testament clearly teaches that each person is competent and free to come to God for himself. No intermediary is needed. No priest or any other person, no creed, or ceremony, no church or anything else is to be placed between an individual and his approach to God. He must be free to believe or not believe, accept or reject, obey or refuse to obey according to his conscience.

This doctrine excludes all interferences with the personal freedom an individual has in his relation to God. It excludes infant baptism and every form of proxy religion. It relies on the Holy Spirit to interpret God's Word.

The doctrine of soul competency demands the recognition and exercise of individual freedom in the government of a church. Each member must be accepted as capable of self-determination and left free to act from inner compulsion. Outward constraint has no place in church government.

Competency of the soul does not mean human self-sufficiency. Neither is man's freedom irresponsible freedom. An individual is competent and free under God. Although God has endowed him with the capacity to think, choose, speak, and act for himself, he must account to God for every thought, choice, spoken word, and deed. Therefore, as he participates in the life and government of his church, he is to seek to know and conform to the will of God. In doing so, he must be careful that in the exercise of his freedom he does not infringe upon the rights of another. He will grant to every other member the freedom he demands for himself.

VI. Each Church, an Autonomous, Spiritual Democracy

Since a church is composed of competent, free individuals, the church itself must be competent and free. Each church stands alone in its relation to God. For this reason no hierarchy or church court is needed. The individual church is completely independent of every other church and denominational body. In other words, each one in autonomous, or self-governing. Any hierarchal structure or order of priesthood is incompatible with the New Testament doctrine of the church. The apostolic churches were sovereign and independent.

Christ, the founder of the church, is its only ruler, and therefore has all authority in and over it. Under him each church is completely free to determine its doctrines, its polity, its leaders, its worship, and its practices. Under him, the government of a church is to be by the consent of the governed.

Within the church, the members practice spiritual democracy. Opportunity is provided for matters to be freely discussed. After seeking through prayer to know the will of God, decisions are made by the congregation.

Church officers are not rulers but servants. They are elected to office by the church and hold office by consent of the church. This is in contrast to churches under a polity which takes the government from the people and places it at ascending levels of authority.

A congregation works voluntarily. Compulsion comes from within, not from coercion without. The practice of voluntariness is essential to the maintenance of spiritual democracy within an autonomous church.

VII. A Church, a Regenerated Membership

The New Testament teaches that regeneration is necessary to salvation and that salvation precedes baptism and church membership. Regeneration takes place when an individual repents of his sins and confesses his faith in Christ. This means that members of a church have been "generated" again, or "born again." They are new creatures (creations) in Christ. Christ is now lord of their lives, and the Holy Spirit dwells within them to guide and empower them, to interpret God's will, and to create a desire to live a holy life.

Regeneration gives man a new nature. It makes him conscious that he has a new relation with God. He now has a holy Father and is the recipient of the spiritual blessings and privileges that his sonship brings. He is made aware that he is to be obedient to God. His first act of obedience is baptism by immersion into a New Testament church, symbolizing his experience of regeneration. As a member of the church, he develops a growing concept of his personal privileges and responsibilities of church membership.

All regenerated members of a church form an organism of living parts so related to one another as to achieve a oneness in Christ. The church is his body. Since Christ cannot be divided, unity must prevail among the members. This unity exists when all who make up his body have had a common experience of regenerating grace, hold common doctrinal beliefs, and feel a common inner compulsion to do his will. This unity strengthened by mutual love for Christ, gives to the members a strong spiritual affinity for one another.

Regeneration is the basis of unity in a church. Only when there is unity can there be true spiritual democracy —government by the people under God.

VIII. EQUAL RIGHTS AND PRIVILEGES OF CHURCH MEMBERS

Each person has worth in the sight of God. There is no difference in the measure of the Father's love and concern for his children. Each has a free, personal relationship with him and is directly responsible to him and to none other. As competent, free, regenerated persons, under God, each receives from him equal rights and privileges.

Nowhere in the New Testament do we find the apostles, elders (pastors), or deacons considered as superior to other Christians. These men served in positions of leadership, but they were regarded as servants or ministers. This same principle must prevail in any church seeking to be true to the New Testament ideal.

Ministers are called to lead, preach, and teach. Deacons and other church officers are elected to positions of leadership, but none are elected to govern. Equal rights and privileges cannot exist when one person, or a group of persons, has authority over others.

Equality of rights and privileges places serious obligations on the members of a church. While enjoying his personal rights and privileges, a member must work to see that every other member enjoys the same freedom. As a regenerated Christian he will heed Paul's admonition: "In lowliness of mind let each esteem other better than themselves. Look not every man on his own things, but every man on the things of others" (Phil. 2:3–4).

This principle takes into account the difference in intelligence, talents, abilities, wealth and influence of members. Though it is true that all stand on a plane of spiritual equality in rights and privileges, members will recognize that "unto whomsoever much is given, of him shall be much required: and to whom men have committed much, of him they will ask the more" (Luke 12:48). Those who are endowed with qualities of leadership and are elected to offices in church government may be expected to contribute more significantly. Even so, these leaders will always have the principle of equal rights and privileges fixed firmly in their minds.

IX. Church Co-operation, a Voluntary Matter

The principle of the autonomy of the church places each church directly under the lordship of Christ, the guidance of the Holy Spirit, and the teaching of the New Testament.

No other authority is recognized other than these. To maintain this position, each church rejects any and all organic ties with any other church or denominational body. It is to be a complete, independent, and self-governing entity.

While maintaining their independency, the churches of the New Testament recognized the existence of areas of interdependency. They felt the need for mutual aid as they faced adversity and persecution. They felt the need for conference as they sought to clarify their doctrines and build their churches. They knew it was expedient that they work together if they were to carry out Christ's commission. The churches felt a kinship with one another which created a desire for Christian fellowship. Through the leading of the Holy Spirit, these early churches were drawn to work together with a deep sense of interdependency and unity.

Several instances are recorded in the New Testament which illustrate the voluntary co-operation of the first churches. The Jerusalem conference, to which churches sent messengers, is perhaps the best example of the churches voluntarily co-operating in seeking a solution to a grave doctrinal problem. The decision reached was accepted by all in a sense of unity of faith and action.

The churches combining their contributions to send aid to the Jerusalem church and the support Paul received as he conducted the missionary journeys are two other examples of co-operative endeavor.

In addition to setting forth the New Testament principle of co-operation among the churches, these illustrations also point up the fact that in their co-operation each church maintained its autonomy. There is no indication of any attempt to dictate or to control. There was no delegation of authority or surrender of independence. From these examples of the practices of the early churches, the conclusion must be drawn that churches of like faith and order should work together in a spirit of voluntary co-operation within the framework of the New Testament polity.

X. Religious Liberty, an Inalienable Right

Religious liberty is essential to the full exercise of the other principles of New Testament polity. The acknowledgment of the sovereignty of God, the lordship of Christ, the guidance of the Holy Spirit, the supreme authority of the Bible, the competency and freedom of the individual, the limitation of church membership to regenerated persons, the autonomy of the church, and the voluntary co-operation of churches demand the right to full religious liberty. Just as the teachings of the New Testament repudiate all forms of ecclesiastical control, they likewise repudiate any control or interference of the state in religion. There is to be a free church and a free state and the enjoyment of soul freedom by the individual in relation to both.

Religious liberty is a term used to denote the relation of an individual, church, or other religious body to the state in matters of religion. It means the right to believe and to worship according to the dictates of conscience, or to disbelieve and not engage in worship if the individual chooses. A person has a right to choose his religion—Catholic, Protestant, Jewish—or he may choose to be a heretic or an atheist. This right and privilege is given him by God. The state is neither to interfere nor to give preferential treatment; all men are to be equal before the law. Furthermore, an individual, church or other religious body has the right to assemble and to communicate their religious beliefs without hindrance or interference as long as they do not violate the rights of others.

The separation of church and state requires that the state be just as free and separate from the church as the church is free and separate from the state. The ideal is a free church and a free state in a free society. Neither is to interfere in the affairs of the other. The state is to recognize the authority and freedom of the church in its spiritual functions and to protect it in the full exercise of this authority and freedom.

The church, in turn, is to recognize the authority and freedom of the state in civil and secular matters. It is to obey the laws of the state in the management of its temporal affairs. If the laws of a state contradict what a congregation believes to be the will of God, it is bound to submit to his sovereignty and obey him, even if it means suffering the penalties of civil authority.

These, then are the New Testament principles of polity. The difference in the divergent types of polity in existence today are due primarily to the underlying concept of the importance and relevance of the New Testament in determining church polity. On one hand is the view that the New Testament clearly sets forth the principles and ideals of polity and that a church is to accept and practice these as authoritative and final. Southern Baptists hold this view.

On the other hand is the belief that the New Testament churches developed a polity that was expedient in their day. The principles they set forth may be adapted, changed, or added to in keeping with the demands of a progressing, changing civilization. Other views range between these two.

Baptists do not believe that polity is a question of expedience but of obedience—obedience to the Word of God. For them New Testament principles of polity do not change. They were ordained of God, taught by Christ, practiced by the first churches, and recorded in the Scriptures.

CHAPTER 3

I. THE INDIVIDUALITY OF MEMBERS IN A CHURCH
   1. Supreme Value of Each Member
   2. Competency of Each Member
   3. Personal Freedom of Each Member

II. THE EQUALITY OF MEMBERS IN A CHURCH
   1. Equality of Rank
   2. Equality of Privileges
   3. Equality of Opportunity

III. THE RESPONSIBILITIES OF MEMBERS IN A CHURCH
   1. Responsible for the Freedom and Rights of Others
   2. Responsible for Participation in Church Government
   3. Responsible for Abiding by Majority Decisions
   4. Responsible for Self-Discipline

3

Church Members' Responsibility for Government

THERE IS NO PLACE for the autocracy of one individual or for an oligarchy of a group of individuals. There is no overlord in a Baptist church. The pastor is neither priest nor bishop, neither dictator nor boss. Rather, he is the servant and leader of the congregation. Deacons are neither to legislate nor to regulate. No individual or group of individuals have power other than to recommend or to use such authority as may have been delegated to them by the church for a particular task. Even when such authority is delegated, supreme and final authority resides in the congregation. When this authority is usurped by one person or by a group, that church ceases to practice Baptist polity.

All leaders of a Baptist church are elected by the church. They are at all times and in all things to be subject to the will of the church. As members, each one has one voice and one vote, no more and no less. This principle does not downgrade the importance of any one individual; instead, it upgrades the importance of all individuals.

I. THE INDIVIDUALITY OF MEMBERS IN A CHURCH

In the practices of Baptist polity the individuality of the members of a church is to be cherished and carefully protected. In the expression of this individuality in the government of a church, each member is to be recognized as of supreme value, competent, and free.

James L. Sullivan wrote:

Baptists are by nature individualists. . . . Under God, each person is given strengths and abilities different from everyone else. Are we to doubt God's wisdom in this creative act? Rather, are we not to conclude that each life has its own particular and distinctive type of service to give?

In our Baptist democracy it is doubtful that we can survive, much less prosper, unless we maintain our emphasis upon individuality. This is what produces creativity, initiative, and determination. It makes for discussion, debate, intelligent evaluation, and balanced decisions.[1]

1. *Supreme Value of Each Member*

Since each person is of infinite worth in the sight of God, the individuality of man must be respected, protected, and developed. His personality must be considered sacred. He is never to become simply a name on the church roll or a face lost in a mass of faces. A church sins against the individual and against God if this is permitted to happen.

Individual differences must be taken into account, however. There will be educational, economic, and social differences as well as age, sex, and personality differences. These differences are neither to be discounted nor neglected, but accepted. Certainly no attempt it to be made to cast all members in the same mold. This is not possible nor is it desirable. Individual differences among the members give a church diversity that in turn contributes strength and vigor to its activities. It is in the plan and will of God that these differences exist.

Just because persons are different they should not be categorized as either inferior or superior. All should be counted worthy of consideration and respect. A true spiritual democracy can be sustained only where a person is accepted for what he is and for what, under God, he can become.

[1] "On Being Ourselves," *News Letter*, V (October, 1961), 2.

2. *Competency of Each Member*

God has given to each person the capacity to be competent in religion. When he becomes a Christian and unites with a church, he is to begin to participate actively in the government of his church. Under the lordship of Christ and the guidance of the Holy Spirit, even a child is capable of determining what he should say and do. Through indoctrination and training in the life and work of the church, he grows in ability to participate more intelligently.

Sometimes an adult member will question the wisdom of permitting children the right to vote. He may observe that a child tends to vote as his parents do. Another may make the accusation that parents sometimes deliberately bring their children to a business meeting with instructions as to how to vote and that a close decision is decided by the votes of these children. While we recognize that children tend to vote with their parents and that some parents may at times violate the rights of their children, every member, regardless of age, must be considered competent and free to vote. The solution to this problem is in the careful teaching and training of both children and parents as to the privilege of voting in a church. As long as a church is truly democratic, the judgments of even the youngest member are to be respected.

The acceptance and practice of the doctrine of soul competency makes for democracy in a church. By continuous consent and active participation of all members, a church's democratic polity is nourished and sustained.

3. *Personal Freedom of Each Member*

Freedom is a cherished heritage of Baptists. The essential expression of the priesthood of the believer lies in its meaning. It means more than the absence of restraint or compulsion; it means the privilege and opportunity to release the God-given powers within each person to think, speak, choose, and act for himself. A Baptist church should deliberately make possible the maximum expression of freedom that each member enjoys in Christ.

The very heart of personal freedom is self-determination. To deny a person the freedom to determine for himself what he considers the highest good is to deny the sacredness of human personality. It is this quality of being free to make rational choices, to know what is good and what is bad, and to decide which to seek that lifts man above all other creatures. While a church through its preaching, teaching, and training seeks to influence and persuade in the direction of the likeness of Christ, it must never coerce or in any way violate the principle of personal freedom.

In churches that limit or simply tolerate individual freedom, a Christian is restricted in the exercise of his competency under God. Leaders should be cautious not to infringe upon the freedom of a member to make his own choices and to determine his own course of action. As long as his choices, decisions, and actions do not violate the voted policies of the church or the freedom of others, he should be free in exercising them. Leaders also should avoid coercive tactics, whether direct or indirect. Assessments of dues, public embarrassment of members not conforming or responding to plans and programs have no place in a church. Participation must always be on a voluntary basis if personal freedom is to be preserved.

An important by-product of personal freedom in a church is that it become a basis of Christian growth and of church development. When freedom of inquiry and discussion exists, there is greater possibility of separating truth from error. Also, there is the probability of discovering better ways of carrying out the programs of a church.

On the other hand, the denial of personal freedom can cause frustration, create suspicion, stifle progress, and encourage authoritarianism.

II. THE EQUALITY OF MEMBERS IN A CHURCH

Each member of a Baptist church shares an equality with every other member. As a body composed of regenerated individuals, a church recognizes that each person shares a common nature with every other member. All are worthy in God's sight. All have become a part of the church in the same way. Every member should have equality of rank, privileges, and opportunity.

1. *Equality of Rank*

Equality of rank in a church does not mean that there are to be no leaders. There are to be officers but no official governing powers. Leaders who have the confidence and respect of the members will generally exert more influence than those who do not. They have the responsibility of being good stewards of their influence.

Equality of rank eliminates any orders in the ministry. This is one reason Baptists insist on congregational polity. "Even the pastor, whom the Holy Spirit makes the overseer, cannot exclude the least significant member. As a member of the local church his rank is precisely that of every other member. 'Orders' in the ministry are unscriptural and 'orders' from the pastor are unauthorized." [2]

2. *Equality of Privileges*

Just as all members are of equal rank in a church, all possess equal privileges. In a Baptist democracy, no one should be permitted to gain ascendancy over others.

---

[2] George W. McDaniel, *The Churches of the New Testament* (Nashville: The Sunday School Board of the Southern Baptist Convention, 1921), p. 25.

Rather, the privileges of one member are to be considered as sacred as those of all other members and so are protected. Each member should feel free to question or disagree with those who make recommendations, whether the recommendations come from the floor, from a committee chairman, or from the pastor.

In a Baptist church, there is to be equality of privilege in expressing one's views. Although a member may be the only one to hold a certain view, he has the right to express it. He also has the privilege of bringing any matter he desires before the congregation for consideration and action. This does not mean that one person's view or recommendation will be equally as valid as another's. Rarely will this be true. Rather, it means that each member has an equal right with every other member to express himself. The church in turn has the right to accept or reject each matter presented to it.

Each member of a Baptist church has the privilege of voting. Equality of privilege of voting means that each member is to be given the opportunity to vote. Voting privileges in a Baptist church are not determined by age or any consideration other than membership. The youngest member has just as much right to vote as the oldest one. The newest member has as much right to vote as the charter member.

It should be obvious that there are to be no conflicts in the equality of privileges. These end for one member at the point they begin to infringe on the rights of any other member. For example, the questions may be asked: What about the member who seems to have been "born in the negative mood and in the objective case" and who is always demanding to be heard? If a church is plagued with such a person, isn't it best just to go ahead and take action without discussion in a business meeting?

It is never best to violate the democratic principles that

should prevail in a Baptist church. If a church is "plagued" with such a member, he must be accepted and his privileges respected. Usually, a moderator who follows good parliamentary procedure can limit the time allowed to such a member while at the same time encourage discussion from other members. Equality of privilege breaks down when one member monopolizes a discussion.

3. *Equality of Opportunity*

Closely related to the equality of rank and privileges is the equality of opportunity. It is because one person ranks equally with every other person and because all have equal privileges that a member possesses equality of opportunity. This means that a person must be able to express his individuality. It eliminates any attempt to mold persons into a particular pattern of thought or action. This does not mean that individual differences are to be obscured or neglected. They are to be given opportunity of expression. Utilizing these differences can help in building the church. Paul looked upon individual differences as "diversities of gifts" and taught that each person has a distinct and important function to perform in the church. He said, in substance, that God has taken all members, each with a different personality, capacities, and abilities, and "hath tempered the body together, having given more abundant honour to that part which lacked: that there should be no schism in the body; but that the members should have the same care one for another" (1 Cor. 12:24-25).

Opportunity to express one's individuality demands equality of opportunity to serve. In a democracy, no qualified member should be arbitrarily excluded from a place of leadership in his church. Official positions should not be reserved for the best educated, the most capable, the most influential, or, even the best trained and most experienced. Instead, a church through prayer and the guidance of the Holy Spirit should seek the persons God would have serve. Individual qualifications are not to be overlooked. But every member of a Baptist church is to be considered capable of serving God within the limits of his abilities and is to be given the opportunity to do so.

J. N. Barnette, former secretary of the Sunday School Department of the Sunday School Board, made many significant contributions toward the progress of Southern Baptist Sunday schools. One of these was to focus the attention of church leaders upon the God-implanted abilities for leadership dormant within every church. He emphasized that any church has in its membership a sufficient number of workers to fill every leadership position if they are enlisted and given the opportunity to exercise their potentialities.

Complete equality of all members includes access to information concerning the administration of the church. Any request for information by any member of the church should be honored. The only exception would be if the information requested would breach another member's rights. For example, a member is entitled to know about the receipts and expenditures of the church, but he has no right to information about an individual's record of contributions, especially if it is understood in a church that giving records are confidential.

Sometimes there is the tendency for staff members, deacons, committees, and others to become secretive and to withhold information from the church. Even when this is done with the best of intentions, it is not democratic. Leaders in a church are elected by the church and are therefore responsible to it. The only time they have the right to keep their discussions and work confidential is when they have been authorized to do so by the church.

There can be no government by the people when the people are kept ignorant.

III. THE RESPONSIBILITIES OF MEMBERS IN A CHURCH

In a democracy every individual freedom, privilege, and opportunity carries with it a corresponding responsibility. When an individual unites with a Baptist church, he voluntarily binds himself with the other members in a common faith and a common purpose. He is now obligated to work with his fellow members for the achievement of the church's goals.

1. *Responsible for the Freedom and Rights of Others*

The Christian is his brother's keeper. Paul admonished the members of the churches of Galatia to "use not liberty for an occasion to the flesh, but by love serve one another" (Gal. 5:13). Among other things, this means that personal liberty is to be subordinated to the needs of others. Recognizing this great truth, George W. McDaniel wrote, "The highest exercise of a right is to surrender that right to the good of others."[3]

In congregational government it is imperative that each member practice self-restraint in the exercise of his individual rights. His chief interest must be the common good, not selfish personal benefits. What is best for the church in its effort to do the will of Christ should be the criterion for his actions.

In his responsibility to protect the freedom and rights of others, a church member should avoid the exercise of individual or group pressures. He should not be involved in any attempt to cover up or to use evasive tactics. If he knows of the existence of such, he should expose them.

---

[3] *Ibid.*, p. 223.

Responsibility for the freedom and rights of others includes the strong helping to strengthen the weak. In every church there are immature Christians. There are also some who feel inferior and tend to withdraw. Others are inclined to let leaders, or those they respect, think and act for them. It is the responsibility of the strong and experienced not to ignore these people, but to help them. They should be patient with them and try to draw them into the activities of the church.

2. *Responsible for Participation in Church Government*

In the twelfth chapter of both Romans and 1 Corinthians Paul describes how even the weakest member is essential to the functioning of the whole. No member should consider lightly his responsibility for speaking and voting his personal convictions concerning the policies and actions of his church. It has been said that not to vote is a half vote for and a half vote against. Far too many church members are casting half votes in opposition to the will of God by not attending the business meetings of their churches.

Church government is not something a church member can leave to others. The priesthood of the believer prohibits the transfer of personal responsibility. Even though a member may believe in the dedication and abilities of those who lead, he cannot escape his personal responsibility to participate. Democracy rests on the active participation of the majority and degenerates when left to the minority.

Church members are responsible for keeping themselves informed concerning the business of their church. They should listen to announcements, read carefully the information mailed into their homes, and attend the meetings in which business is transacted. In these meetings they should ask questions about things they do not understand. They should speak out and give voice to their convictions, whether for or against. They should use their God-given freedom and rights to help determine the governmental affairs of the church.

3. Responsible for Abiding by Majority Decisions

Although each member has the privilege of speaking his beliefs and casting his vote in all matters of church business, the decision of the majority is final. When an action is voted, that action stands unless the congregation itself, in another vote, cancels or changes it. The members constitute the body of Christ, and he reigns as head. Therefore, there is no higher authority to change or rescind the action voted by a Baptist church. The principle of the autonomy of the church prevails.

A majority vote does not necessarily mean that the majority is right and the minority wrong. Men are fallible in a church as elsewhere. Yet it has pleased Christ to entrust the business of his church to its members. He holds the members responsible for seeking, knowing, and doing his will. This calls for searching the Scriptures, for prayer, and for dedication. A church is less likely to make mistakes when a majority submits to the will of Christ.

Although majority decisions must prevail in church actions, this is by no means the ideal.

In the light of New Testament teaching, the true ideal of church action is unanimity. Majority rule should not be employed as the prevailing practice but the last resort. Every honorable recourse should be exhausted to secure unanimous action before the prerogative of the majority is exercised. There are three courses of action to be followed in church deliberations. The one to be sought first and eagerly is unanimity; failing of this, the minority can yield to the judgment of the majority and vote to make an action unanimous; if the minority for reasons sufficient to themselves must remain irreconcilable, then the voice of the majority must prevail—*as a last resort.*[4]

When a congregation votes its decision on a matter, it is the duty of every member to accept and abide by this decision. If there is not a unanimous vote, the minority is just as responsible as the majority to act in accord with the action of the church. This also applies to any who were not present when the voting took place.

In a spiritual democracy all members labor together for God. If in good conscience, devoid of all selfish interest, a member cannot do so, he should quietly refrain. By no means should he say or do anything deliberately designed to block or influence others against the action voted by the church. If he feels compelled to reopen the matter in a business meeting of the church, he may do so provided he follows the approved procedures.

4. *Responsible for Self-Discipline*

In the government of a Baptist church there should be no coercion. For the most part, the only discipline exercised should be self-discipline. Under the lordship of Christ, the guidance of the Holy Spirit, and the teaching of God's Word, a Christian is to order his life so as to preserve the harmony and spiritual fellowship of his church. He should always exercise self-control and consideration for others. He must lay aside selfish interests and seek to do what is best for the body of Christ. He should co-operate, as long as he can do so in good conscience, to the limits of his ability in carrying out every action voted by his church.

Through the practice of self-discipline it is possible for

[4] H. E. Dana and L. M. Sipes, *A Manual of Ecclesiology* (Kansas City, Kansas: Central Seminary Press, 1944), p. 228.

members to disagree, debate, vote majority and minority decisions, and at the same time retain their love and respect for one another. They learn that they can be on opposite sides of an issue without becoming enemies and that they can express their views and vote their convictions without fear of reprisals or loss of friendships.

The measure to which a church keeps the individuality, equality, and responsibility of its members at the center of thought and action is the measure to which a church will be able to maintain congregational polity. To the degree that a church loses sight of these fundamentals it will move in the direction of a more authoritarian polity. The members of a church are of primary importance; their form of government is secondary.

CHAPTER 4

I. A CHURCH—AN ENTITY
   1. Complete Within Itself
   2. Unified in Christ
   3. Equal with Every Other Church

II. A CHURCH—AUTONOMOUS
   1. Free of Ecclesiastical Ties
   2. Independent of All Other Bodies
   3. Congregational in Government

III. A CHURCH—CONGREGATIONAL DEMOCRACY
   1. Determines Its Membership
   2. Determines Its Programs
   3. Determines Its Organization
   4. Determines Its Leaders

4

A Church and Its Government

CHRIST DID NOT concern himself with the actual governmental structure of his church while on earth. As long as he was physically present, the church was directly under his divine headship. After his ascension the Holy Spirit came to guide the church in its development. It soon had elders (pastors) and deacons. It had requirements for membership. It met for worship and for the observance of the Lord's Supper. It launched a program of missions. Other churches were established and similarly organized. Beginning with the Jerusalem conference, the churches began to co-operate voluntarily in the kingdom enterprise.

Although the New Testament does not give detailed information concerning the government of a church, it does contain doctrinal principles with which church government must harmonize. These principles are changeless and are to be paramount in the development of a church's governmental structure.

I. A CHURCH—AN ENTITY

The evidence is abundant and conclusive that the first churches were individual, separate, and independent of one another. They were unquestionably complete within themselves.

1. *Complete Within Itself*

A church has a distinctiveness in its relation to the kingdom. The kingdom of God, the kingdom of Christ, and the kingdom of heaven are one and the same. It is a spiritual kingdom over which Christ reigns. All of the redeemed of Christ are in spiritual union with him and with one another in the kingdom.

But whereas the kingdom embraces all believers, it does not embrace all churches in some form of super union. The two are different in nature and in function. The kingdom is invisible; the church is visible. The kingdom is a theocracy; the church is a democracy (under God). The church has a form of organization and a system of government; the kingdom does not. The church is an individual active body commissioned by Christ to bring men into his kingdom. The kingdom expresses the relationship which men have to Christ and with one another.

The church is individual, distinctive, and autonomous. It is an integral body, a whole. It is not a part of some larger body. It exists as an entity, separate and apart.

2. Unified in Christ

Although a church needs organization, it is more than an organization. It is an organism. It is composed of human beings, who make up the spiritual body of Christ. Paul wrote to the Corinthians "The body is one, and hath many members, and all the members of that one body, being many are one body: so also is Christ. . . . Now ye are the body of Christ, and members in particular" (1 Cor. 12:12, 27). He also told this church that although the members had different gifts and different functions, all were of one body.

A church does not find its unity in Christ through an ecclesiastical linkage to a hierarchical or an oligarchical head, but in a direct and vital relationship to Christ himself. This unity is strengthened through common doctrinal beliefs held by the members. Theirs is a "unity of the faith, and of the knowledge of the Son of God" (Eph.

4:13). Any attempt at unity within a church which does not grow out of a common faith and common beliefs will be superficial and meaningless.

It is recorded of the early Christians: "The multitude of them that believed were of one heart and of one soul" (Acts 4:32). This is the ideal spiritual unity that Christ would have prevail in each of his churches. Unity of heart and soul is the only unity that will enable a church to advance Christ's kingdom. It is through a local congregation that unity can have full and adequate expression.

The unifying factor in a church is love—love for Christ and for one another. Paul describes the attributes of love in the thirteenth chapter of 1 Corinthians. When this kind of love controls a church, there will be unity of thought, feeling, and action; there will be the sacrificial giving of self in the service of others. Only through love are the members of a church able to subordinate their selfish interests and govern themselves for the common good. When love is lacking, rivalry, strife, and personal aggrandizement are inevitable.

Christ was so concerned that his followers love one another that he told them, "A new commandment I give unto you, That ye love one another; as I have loved you, that ye also love one another" (John 13:34). When church members, who believe alike, have this kind of love for one another, their unity will be genuine and vital.

3. Equal with Every Other Church

Individual churches are equal just as individuals within churches are equal. It is not the will of Christ that one church have supremacy over another church.

The church at Jerusalem naturally had the love and respect of the other churches. It was the church from which members first went out to organize new churches. Yet the Jerusalem church did not attempt to dictate to even the smallest of these new struggling churches. The evidence in the Scriptures is that there was an acknowledgment of equality among these churches with each respecting the sovereignty and independence of the others.

Baptists pattern their churches after New Testament churches. They believe in and practice the equality of churches. One expression of this is in the contention for equality of churches along with the freedom of churches in the state. Baptists are rigidly opposed to a state church or a privileged church within a state.

The relationship Baptist churches have with one another in denominational co-operation is another expression of this belief. All churches have equal opportunity to receive the benefits that denominational affiliation affords. More important, all churches have equal opportunity to give support to the world mission program for which the denominational bodies exist.

All churches may send messengers to the annual meetings of the association, the state convention, and the Southern Baptist Convention. All messengers enjoy equal rights and privileges in these meetings. In keeping with the constitutional provisions and parliamentary procedures, each messenger may recommend, discuss, and vote.

There is a difference in the number of messengers churches are entitled to send to annual meetings of denominational bodies. But this does not invalidate the principle of equality of churches. It does just the opposite. There would be no equality if a church of sixty members could send the same number of messengers as a church of six thousand members, or if a church which gave only a few dollars to world missions could send the same number of messengers as a church that gave several thousand dollars. These restrictions and allowances make for equality rather than destroy it.

A further safeguard to equality is the limitation each

of the denominational bodies has on the number of messengers from any one church. The maximum number is low enough to keep messengers from one or a few large churches from being in the majority. It also keeps the annual meetings of the denominational bodies from becoming excessively large and a hindrance to carrying on business effectually.

Maintaining the equality of churches should be of concern to every Baptist. The elevation of one church above another in thought, even if not in practice, is contrary to the teachings of Christ.

II. A CHURCH—AUTONOMOUS

In the treatment of the principle of the autonomy of a New Testament church, it was stated that each church stands alone in relation to God and is completely free to determine its doctrines, polity, and leaders. This means that a church practices self-determination in the government of its affairs. There are several characteristics of an autonomous church. It is (1) free of ecclesiastical ties; (2) independent of all other bodies; and (3) congregational in government.

1. *Free of Ecclesiastical Ties*

The only ties a Baptist church has with another church, association, or convention are ties of doctrinal beliefs, fellowship, and the desire to co-operate voluntarily in missions and other denominational activities. No organizational or governmental ties whatsoever exist. Yet members from churches go as messengers to compose the membership of the denominational bodies in their annual conventions. Some of these are elected to serve as officers and as members of boards and committees. Executives and other employees of denominational agencies are members and often leaders in churches.

2. *Independent of All Other Bodies*

To be autonomous a church must also be independent. The first step toward the surrender of autonomy is to become dependent upon another body. For this reason each Baptist church owns its own property and pays the salaries of its employees. It insists on the equality of churches and denominational bodies and contends for separation of church and state.

Sometimes it may be necessary in the first months of the existence of a new church for another church or denominational body to provide a supplement for the pastor's salary or to meet payments on a building. While this arrangement exists, a church cannot be completely autonomous. Independence will bring it autonomy.

In its independence a church should not lose sight of its interdependency. A church can affiliate with denominational groups and co-operate in the work fostered by them without surrendering its independency of decision, choice, or action. As seen in the New Testament principle of co-operation, it is expedient for a church to work with other churches in seeking to carry out the commission of Christ. In this way it can do its own work well while joining with others in carrying out the worldwide task of the church. It can do this without compromising its autonomy or weakening the autonomy of co-operating churches.

3. *Congregational in Government*

It is not enough for a church to be independent of all outside controls. To be completely autonomous it must make sure that within the church, control is actually in the hands of the congregation. In other words, congregational polity is not just a principle; it is to be a reality. With the high rate of mobility of people, church membership sometimes changes rapidly. Often this results in more authority being delegated to, or assumed by, long-standing members. While it is commendable for new members to wait until they are better acquainted and informed before feeling competent to express themselves in a business meeting, they should be encouraged to participate. As soon as a person unites with a Baptist church, he is obligated to take part in the work of that church just as are those who have been members for years. When only a few are inclined to speak, and thereby influence the decision of a congregation, the church is in danger of drifting away from the practice of democratic government.

Coupled with the accelerated rate of change in church memberships is the growing size and complexity of organizations and activities in churches. Actually, there may develop many "congregations" within the larger congregation. The natural tendency then is for each to move in the direction of organizational autonomy. To avoid this some churches have delegated or allowed authority to slip into the hands of the pastor, the deacons, or both. This is centralization of authority, which is detrimental to democratic government in a church.

The extent to which a church is autonomous in practice as well as in theory depends upon the pastor and other church leaders. They should be familiar with the principles of New Testament polity in order to guide the church in practicing them.

III. A Church—Congregational Democracy

Congregational democracy means that a church's government is the direct responsibility of the congregation. There is every evidence that Christ placed authority in the membership of a church as a whole and meant for it to remain there. It is therefore incumbent on each Baptist congregation to hold tenaciously to the reins of government and to see that no individual or group of individuals, in the church or in any denominational body, makes decisions for, or exercises any jurisdiction over, the church.

Congregational democracy demands regular meetings of the congregation in business session. In these meetings the members are to keep themselves informed about the affairs of the church. They are to discuss matters freely, even debate them, and reach their decisions by voting. They are to determine their membership, programs, organization, and leaders.

1. *Determines Its Membership*

Baptists are agreed that the basis of membership in a church is salvation in Christ and baptism by immersion on the authority of a New Testament church. They readily receive members by transfer of membership from other Baptist churches, or by statement, if a letter cannot be secured. Occasionally a member excluded from the membership will be received by restoration. By whatever means an individual may apply for membership, the decision of whether or not he is received rests with the church.

Traditionally Baptists have received members into their churches by voting in a congregational meeting. It may be in a Sunday worship service, a mid-week prayer service, or a night during a revival. Some churches have the policy of receiving members only in a business meeting. Usually letters of dismissal are granted in business meetings. Names of members uniting with churches of other denominations are also removed from the roll by vote of the church in business meeting.

Questions have been raised about the validity of churches perfunctorily voting on new members. At one extreme is a church that receives all who come, without actually voting. At the other is a church that has rigid requirements, including a waiting period, instructions, and a commitment to statement of will's and won't's. In between these two extremes most churches adopt a procedure for receiving members into their fellowship. Each church has the right to determine its own membership requirements.

Determining qualifications for membership includes not only receiving members but also maintaining them. A church has the authority to exclude or discipline members just as it has the authority to receive them. Christ aware of the power of sin and desiring that his church keep itself free of defilement, gave the procedure to follow. In Matthew 18:15-17; Romans 16:17; and 1 Corinthians 5:9-13 both the responsibility and the authority are placed clearly upon the church first to seek the restoration of an offending member. If this fails, the offender is to be disciplined more severely, even to the extent of expulsion. A church must exercise this authority with extreme caution and in the spirit of love, but it should do so nevertheless.

Once a church takes such an action, there is no higher authority to which a member may appeal. The church has the authority to receive the member by restoration, but no other church or denominational body has the right to recommend that it do so. Of course, another church may receive him into its membership by statement, but this is a rare procedure.

2. Determines Its Programs

Southern Baptist churches have developed similarity in their programs and activities. So close is this similarity that it borders on uniformity. A calendar of suggested activities is prepared and circulated by the officers of the association, state convention, and the Southern Baptist Convention. A church affiliated with all three of these denominational bodies then determines which activities it will place in its programs.

In determining its programs, a church will wish to co-operate with each of the denominational bodies. Yet the church must not neglect the needs of its own members and the community in which it is located. Therefore, a pastor will perhaps work with a church council in determining well-balanced programs including both local and denominational activities. After presentation, discussion, and adoption by the church, they become the programs of the church.

Each church determines its programs. Denominational bodies may recommend, but the church decides. Any attempt to coerce a church to participate in any phase of a denominational program is completely out of harmony with Baptist polity. A church must always be able to determine its own programs without any interference or fear of criticism.

3. *Determines Its Organization*

Baptist churches vary in size from less than fifty to several thousand members. They meet in buildings ranging from one room to over a hundred. Their missions and operating budgets vary. One church may be taking its first steps in growing from a mission into a church. Another may be celebrating its centennial anniversary. One may need a simple organization; another, a complex one.

Organization is the formal arrangement or pattern whereby church members relate themselves to one another for accomplishing the tasks of a church.

Who is to decide the organization that a Baptist church shall have? Only the congregation, by means of its democratic processes, can decide. A church may request the advice or assistance of a denominational leader, but that leader has neither the authority nor the prerogative to tell the church how it must operate. The pastor, deacons, or committees may study and recommend and give leadership to the actual organizing, but the decision as to the structure of the organization rests with the congregation.

Out of practical experiences in the churches, a general pattern of organization has evolved which is distinctive. Beginning with the officers in evidence in the New Testament churches—the pastor and the deacons—churches usually have a clerk, a treasurer, and other general officers considered necessary. Committees have also been found to be essential in the organization of a democratic church. The number of committees in a church should be determined by the areas of work that needs to be done. A small church may have only two or three committees and a large church thirty or more.

Perhaps the rather uniform pattern in the educational organizations of Baptist churches has done as much as anything else to contribute to the similarity of the over-all pattern in the churches of the denomination. Southern Baptist Sunday schools, Training Unions, Brotherhoods, Music Ministries, and Woman's Missionary Unions are distinctive in organization and methods. So extensive and thorough has been the promotion of these organizations that little variation will be found in the churches, except for size and number of units.

Whatever the influence brought to bear on a church, whether by leaders within the membership or leaders of the denomination outside the membership, the congregation should always decide upon its own organization. It will cease to be an independent body if it readily accepts everything brought before it. On the other hand, in making its decision it should do so in a co-operative spirit, whether it decides for or against a proposed plan.

4. *Determines Its Leaders*

In keeping with the New Testament principle of autonomy, each Baptist church determines who will serve as its pastor, deacons, and other leaders. It determines the officers needed: their qualifications and responsibilities; how they are to be nominated and elected; and the tenures of their offices.

It is significant that the first officers elected in the early church were probably deacons. The word "deacon" means servant. The basic responsibility of the deacons in a church is to minister to the needs of the congregation. They are not to rule, decide for, or even to act on behalf of the church, except as they are requested to do so by the church. Thus more and more churches are dropping the designation "board of deacons" and simply using the term "the deacons." Church members accustomed to serving on, or being subservient to, boards of directors in the business world are inclined to associate the idea of a policy-making, ruling body with such a "board" in the church. There are a number of areas in which deacons may serve effectively, but governing the affairs of a church is not one of them.

It is necessary for a pastor to have a measure of authority delegated to him by the church. Without it he cannot exercise oversight as Peter said, or administer the affairs of the church. The church, however, decides "the measure," and the pastor is directly responsible to the church in the exercise of this authority.

When God calls a man to preach, he expects him to find his messages in the Scriptures, under the guidance of the Holy Spirit. No church has the right to tell a pastor what he is to preach. It may counsel him regarding his sermons, but it should do so only with great caution. A church, however, can tell a pastor whether he may preach; for the pulpit belongs to the church, not to the man who occupies it. He preaches from it only by the consent of the people.

In and through preaching a pastor magnifies the authority of the Scriptures. A pastor who preaches on authority of the Scriptures soon is identified as a channel of that authority. This makes it necessary for him always to re-member that this authority is one of enlightenment, per-suasion, and conviction, not of coercion.

By position and preaching, a pastor usually possesses the authority of influence. What he believes and says will usually bear a great deal of weight in influencing the de-cisions of the church. This places a great responsibility on him to depend on the Lord for direction and to empty him-self of personal desires and ambitions. It also demands that he exert extreme care to keep the government of a church centered where it belongs—in the congregation.

What has been said about the pastor applies also to other staff members and volunteer leaders in the church. Each will necessarily need some degree of authority to do the work assigned to him. Both the church and the leaders, however, must always remember that ultimate authority resides in the church. At any time it can overrule or withdraw authority and can remove a person from office or remove the office itself from the structure of its gov-ernment.

CHAPTER 5

I. SOUTHERN BAPTIST DENOMINATIONALISM
   1. The Meaning
   2. The Principles
   3. The System

II. A CHURCH AND DENOMINATIONAL BODIES
   1. Each Composed of Individuals
   2. Each an Autonomous Body
   3. The Primacy of the Church

III. THE GOVERNMENT OF DENOMINATIONAL BODIES
   1. Messengers to the Annual Meetings
   2. Executive Groups Between the Annual Meetings
   3. Executives in the Convention Agencies

5

Denominational Government

GOVERNMENT IN Southern Baptist denominational bodies is determined as far as possible by the same New Testament principles of polity as that of the churches. Primarily for this reason, but also because of close working relationships, it is only natural that a pattern of government common to all three bodies—association, state convention, and Southern Baptist Convention—has developed. Modifications and variations exist, but a messenger to annual meetings of any of these groups will have an understanding of the system of government.

I. SOUTHERN BAPTIST DENOMINATIONALISM

The Sunday School Board printed and distributed twelve tracts (now out of print) called the *Denominational Series*. One was entitled "A True Denominationalism," by E. Y. Mullins. In the Introduction, Mullins stated that he proposed "to show that there is a true and worthy denominationalism." In our age Baptists need to be aware that a Southern Baptist denominationalism exists.

1. *The Meaning*

"There is no such thing as a Southern Baptist Church," someone says occasionally. If the speaker is thinking in terms of a super Southern Baptist Church composed of all individual churches, most Baptists agree. And they would even agree that in the literal sense there are no Southern Baptist churches, for each church is individual and autonomous. In the sense of being affiliated with or in co-operation with the Southern Baptist Convention, there are many Southern Baptist churches. Because of this concept, an increasing number of churches in pioneer areas are adding "Southern" to their names.

It is customary for a denomination to be identified with its national organization whether it is called "Church," as is the practice of those having a form of government which limits the autonomy of local churches, or "Convention," as is the Southern Baptist Convention. Each Baptist, each church, each association, each state convention, and the Southern Baptist Convention comprise the Southern Baptist denomination. To illustrate, a person may be a member of the University Baptist Church of Fort Worth, Texas, a Southern Baptist church. This church is affiliated with the Tarrant Baptist Association—a Southern Baptist association. The church is also affiliated with the Baptist General Convention of Texas, a Southern Baptist state convention and with the national body, the Southern Baptist Convention.

Southern Baptist church and Southern Baptist Convention church are two entirely different designations. The first usage is correct and proper; the second, erroneous. Inserting "Convention" in the name implies two misconceptions of Baptist polity. One is that the church is an organic part of the Convention; the other is that the church is governmentally subservient to the Convention. In either case, the idea conveyed is that the church is subordinate and subject to the Convention.

Neither a church, an association, nor a state convention is organically, organizationally, or governmentally a part of the Southern Baptist Convention. On the contrary, each is separate, independent, and autonomous. However, they are bound together in spirit and share common beliefs, convictions, and purposes. These are the ties that have united Southern Baptists into a denomination of individuals, churches, associations, state conventions, and a national convention.

2. *The Principles*

Jack L. Gritz, editor of the *Baptist Messenger* of Oklahoma, wrote in the August 11, 1960, issue: "Southern Baptists sincerely endeavor to be completely true to the teachings of the Bible in all things. This is the reason for our existence as a separate denomination."

Printed in the August 18 edition, were excerpts from the famous sermon on religious liberty preached by George W. Truett, May 16, 1932, on the steps of the National Capitol, Washington, D.C. In this sermon Truett said: "Ideas rule the world. A denomination is molded by its ruling principles, just as a nation is thus molded and just as individual life is thus molded. Our fundamental essential principles have made our Baptist people."

The fundamental essential principles, as Truett referred to them, are the bedrock of Southern Baptist denominationalism. Without them there could never have been a denomination such as Baptists now have. If these principles are ever compromised, the denomination will cease to exist as it is known today.

The doctrinal principles that bind Southern Baptists together determine their polity. In the area of beliefs about the nature, membership, and polity of the church, Southern Baptists are distinctive. Their strict adherence to the practice of these principles of polity has contributed to Southern Baptist denominationalism.

3. *The System*

The system consists of four united bodies: church, association, state convention, and Southern Baptist Convention. The unity these maintain is not organic unity. Neither is it organizational sequence nor governmental ties. Their unity is one of spirit, conviction, and purpose. It is a unity of association and action, of being in harmony and agreement. Above all, it is a unity of loyalty to Christ and the Bible.

Admittedly, the Southern Baptist denominational system is not the most efficient. The monarchial system of the Roman Catholics has been rated by many efficiency experts as being superior to any organization or government in the world. The episcopal and presbyterian systems are likewise structured for greater efficiency than is possible in a congregational government. But Baptists believe that while efficiency is important, there are other things more important. They refuse to sacrifice or compromise their doctrinal principles for efficiency. Under the lordship of Christ and the guidance of the Holy Spirit, they believe they can achieve the measure of efficiency God wants them to have within the framework of their New Testament principles of polity.

In an article "Genius of Baptist Co-operation," James L. Sullivan wrote:

If the "most efficient" denominational organizational structure were followed, the churches of a given county would have united to make up the association. The associations of a state would have elected delegates to the state conventions and the various state conventions would have jointly made up the Southern Baptist Convention and would therefore have elected the delegates to it. Not so with Southern Baptists—they have expressed fear of such a pyramid form of denominational government which could conceivably produce hierarchical tendencies. . . .

The Southern Baptist plan seems organizationally bunglesome when contrasted with the straight lines of control of a pure hierarchical system where such controls are channeled down to local churches and the local churches have no choice except to abide by the decision dispatched to them.[1]

The principles precede, produce, and control the sys-

[1] *News Letter*, X (January, 1961), 2.

tem. Southern Baptists must be vigilant in keeping the principles and the system of their denomination in this order. As long as this is true, there will continue to be a true and worthy denominationalism.

II. A CHURCH AND DENOMINATIONATIONAL BODIES

A church bulletin described the denomination as a federation of independent democracies. This is not an apt description. Although a federation is established by common agreement, it calls for each unit to subordinate certain of its powers to a central government or authority. This is foreign to the way Baptists govern themselves.

Distinction needs to be made between the terms "Baptist bodies" and "denominational bodies." In general usage, the term "Baptist body" is used when speaking of a church, association, state convention, or the Southern Baptist Convention. The term "denominational body" is generally used to apply to any one of the three general organizations other than the church. Therefore, Baptists think of their denominational system as being composed of the churches and the three denominational bodies. Any further references to Baptist bodies will include churches, but they will not be included in references to denominational bodies. And although some state bodies are known as general associations instead of conventions, they will be referred to as state conventions.

1. *Each Composed of Individuals*

A Baptist church consists of individuals who have been regenerated, baptized, and received by the congregation into its membership. Likewise, each of the three denominational bodies is composed of certain of these same individuals, who may be elected as messengers to the annual meetings. Neither an association, a state convention, nor the Southern Baptist Convention receives messengers from either of the other two denominational bodies. No Baptist body is made up of other Baptist bodies; each is made up of individual church members.

The Southern Baptist Convention is not composed of all the state conventions, and the state conventions are not composed of all the associations within their respective borders. Nor, in the organic sense, are any of the three denominational bodies made up of churches. Each denominational body has as its members the duly elected messengers from the churches to the annual meetings.

"But," someone may ask, "do not the churches petition for membership in the denominational bodies and, after being received, send their messengers to become members of these bodies?" Yes and no. It all depends on the meaning applied to membership. Actually, "affiliation" describes the relationship more correctly than does "membership." If one thinks of affiliate membership, he will not be far from right. But even if a church is considered an affiliate member, it must be remembered that the designation in no way excludes the church's freedom, autonomy, and independence.

Perhaps it is easier to understand how each Baptist body is composed of individuals, instead of other Baptist bodies, when one realizes that the messengers are void of authority. They are what the name implies, messengers, not delegates. The church delegates nothing to them. They are neither permitted to speak nor vote for their churches. They speak and vote as individual members of the annual sessions of the association or convention of which they have become a part. And, in a sense, they return to their churches as messengers from the denominational body to report on the deliberations and actions of the annual meeting.

Baptists reject the "delegate" concept because they believe it infringes on the New Testament principles that each individual is competent and free under God. They adhere to these principles in their churches, and they adhere to them in their denominational meetings. Although churches may sometimes instruct their messengers, they do so in the knowledge that each messenger is free to speak and vote his own convictions.

It is not unusual in annual meetings for messengers from the same church to take opposing stands on an issue. In doing so, each is simply practicing the same principle of equal rights and privileges that he enjoys in his church.

What has been said about personal responsibility of members in a church also applies to messengers. They must not forget that they are messengers from their respective churches. Each one is personally obligated to represent his church in a worthy manner. Each should seek to the best of his ability to know the mind and will of his church. As long as these are compatible with what he believes to be the will of God, he should speak and vote accordingly.

2. Each an Autonomous Body

If associations and conventions are made up of individuals and these individuals are the elected messengers of the churches, do the churches then determine the membership of the other bodies? Indirectly they do. The messengers must first be elected by the churches, but each of the three denominational bodies is the sole authority in determining whether or not it will receive them.

Each association determines the admission of churches into its fellowship. But this does not automatically qualify the messengers from these churches to be members of the association. The association reserves the right to accept or reject any or all who may be elected by a church as its messengers to the annual meeting. This is true also of conventions.

Each denominational body is autonomous in determining both the qualifications of the churches seeking affiliation with it and also the qualifications of the messengers sent by these churches to the annual meetings. For this reason, usually the first order of business in the annual meetings is the recognition and "seating" of messengers from the churches.

An example of a Baptist denominational body exercising its autonomy in determining its membership is the action taken in the 1961 California state convention. There was a movement to lead the convention to vote to recognize messengers from churches having open communion and admitting alien immersion, which the convention constitution forbids. California Baptists voted to continue their constitutional restriction and denied recognition of messengers from these churches.

Each denominational body is autonomous not only in determining its membership but also in every area of government. None has a right to interfere in the affairs of another. When a decision is made by any one of them, it is final. There is no higher ecclesiastical authority that can reverse this decision, alter it, coerce another body to adopt it, or in any way interfere in another's decisions.

The autonomy of each Baptist body is respected because none ranks above another in polity. All are of equal rank. In recognition of this principle of equality of Baptist bodies, the North Carolina Baptist Convention passed a constitutional amendment a few years ago declaring that it "does not claim and will never attempt to exercise any authority over an affiliated church or any other Baptist body."

Baptists avoid using the term "headquarters" when referring to the location of denominational offices. Denominations with other than a democratic polity have their headquarters, but Baptists do not. The term means the center of authority, operations, and control. Baptists do not have such a center.

The Southern Baptist Convention accentuated this in 1956 when it adopted a resolution on its relations with other Baptist bodies. In this resolution the Convention affirmed that "there is no relation of superiority and inferiority among Baptist general [denominational] bodies. All are equal."

The idea of Baptist headquarters is completely incompatible with the autonomy of separate and independent bodies.

3. *The Primacy of the Church*

Although the churches have no greater rank in polity than the other three Baptist bodies, the associations, the state conventions and the Southern Baptist Convention are dependent on the churches. The churches comprise the affiliated memberships, send the messengers to the annual meetings, furnish the finances, and implement the programs. Individual churches are the lifeline of Southern Baptist work.

The churches occupy a primary position in that they elect the messengers who in turn comprise the membership of denominational offices, executive boards, and committees. These messengers also determine programs and the budget appropriations to finance these programs. They have in their power the approval or the rescinding of any action taken by the officers, boards, or committees. The churches are primary because the three denominational bodies are subject to the decisions and actions voted by the messengers from the churches in the annual meetings. James L. Sullivan said in the January, 1961 issue of *News Letter* that "this simply means that the churches through their elected messengers control the work done in all areas of our Baptist organizational life."

III. The Government of Denominational Bodies

In the government of the associations, state conventions, and the Southern Baptist Convention, Baptist polity is unique. A few other denominations practice congregational polity in their churches, but none approximate the variations in polity practiced by Southern Baptists in their denominational bodies.

These range from congregational democracy in the annual meetings of the three general bodies to executive control in each agency. In between is a governing board, and within each agency there are descending ranks of officials. Ultimate authority, however, is always in the hands of the denominational body. Through its own constitution and bylaws and those of its agencies, through its election of members of its controlling boards, and through its annual meetings, there are sufficient checks and balances for it to exercise its authority and keep the agencies under democratic control. For this reason Baptist polity in its totality has congregationalism as its essential quality.

To understand better how polity functions in the denominational bodies it must be seen as it is practiced in the annual denominational meetings, between these meetings, and every day in the agencies.

1. *Messengers to the Annual Meetings*

When an association, state convention, or the Southern Baptist Convention meets in annual session, authority resides in the messengers. Although these messengers come as the elected representatives of their churches, they weld themselves together into an entity.

They cannot forget the identity they have with their churches, but they now have a new identity as active members of the denominational body. As members of this group they enjoy the same freedoms, privileges, and rights they enjoy in their churches. They also find that Baptists govern themselves in denominational meetings much the same as they do in church business meetings.

The conventions have presidents and the associations moderators, each elected in the previous annual meeting. Each presides over the meetings. Each body has a constitution and bylaws by which it controls its actions. Each also has parliamentary rules by which deliberations are controlled. These instruments have been adapted and refined through the years by amendments and additions in order to insure orderliness and democratic control. In a sense, each has a constitutional form of government.

In an editorial preceding the 1961 meeting of the Baptist General Convention of Texas, E. S. James wrote in the *Baptist Standard:* "The primary purpose of the meeting is to give messengers from all the churches an opportunity to voice their convictions and to participate in the whole program of work."

Inspiration and fellowship are important aspects of annual meetings, but conducting denominational business is paramount. The messengers hear reports from the agencies and committees. Discussions and decisions are made on the recommendations. Most of these recommendations are made by the executive boards or committees, but any messenger may bring any matter before the assembled body for discussion and action as long as both the item and the manner in which it is presented is in accord with the constitution and rules by which the body conducts its business. Likewise, any messenger may speak and vote his convictions on any report or motion.

2. Executive Groups Between the Annual Meetings

In presbyterian polity, government in a church is placed in the hands of an elected board of elders of equal rank. Upon their election, a church delegates authority to exercise governmental control during the ensuing year. Baptist denominational bodies do similarly between their annual sessions. The Southern Baptist Convention elects an executive committee and the states and associations elect executive boards. These executive groups carry out the decisions made in the annual meetings and otherwise act for the larger bodies within the allowances and restrictions of their constitutions and bylaws.

In addition to the Executive Committee of the Southern Baptist Convention and the executive boards of the conventions and associations, each convention and some of the larger associations have their agencies and institutions, with each of these having elected boards, directors, or trustees. Usually a person is elected for a term or two terms of a given number of years and then is not eligible for reelection until a year has elapsed.

The agencies of the Convention are: Foreign Mission Board; Home Mission Board; The Sunday School Board; Annuity Board; The Southern Baptist Theological Seminary; The Southwestern Baptist Theological Seminary; New Orleans Baptist Theological Seminary; Golden Gate Baptist Theological Seminary; The Southeastern Baptist Theological Seminary; Midwestern Baptist Theological Seminary; Southern Baptist Hospital (two—New Orleans, Louisiana, and Jacksonville, Florida); Southern Baptist Foundation; The Southern Baptist Commission on the American Baptist Theological Seminary; Brotherhood Commission; The Radio and Television Commission; The Historical Commission; The Christian Life Commission; Education Commission; The Stewardship Commission.

Although owned and controlled by the Southern Baptist Convention, each agency has a governing board and a full-time executive-administrative staff to carry on its work between conventions.

The state convention executive boards (also a few associational executive boards) have broader powers than the Executive Committee of the Southern Baptist Convention. The reason for this is the structural system of checks and balances among the Convention's agencies. Each has a governing board, directors, or trustees elected by the Convention and subject only to the Convention. Each has its own articles of incorporation and constitution and bylaws. The role of the Executive Committee, in addition to acting for the Convention between sessions, works with agency heads in determining an over-all budget. As money is received, it is disbursed to the agencies in keeping with the will of the Convention expressed in its adopted budget. It also works with the agencies in planning a co-ordinated program to recommend to the Convention each year.

3. *Executives in the Convention Agencies*

Delegating administrative authority to an executive officer is a common practice in any type of government. While an executive secretary must have sufficient authority to do the work for which he is responsible, it is authority under controls. In addition to the governing board to which he is responsible, his authority is limited by a constitution and bylaws and by policies and procedures that provide guidelines. Behind both the executive board and the written "laws" is the Convention in which is vested the ultimate authority.

Serving with and under the executive secretary may be a few or many division and department heads. These men must have sufficient powers to do their work. Usually the extent of these powers will be defined in job descriptions. They are subject to the authority of the executive head, just as he is subject to the agency's board and it in turn to the Convention.

CHAPTER 6

I. RELIGIOUS LIBERTY
   1. A Basic Principle
   2. A Gift from God
   3. A Legal Provision of Government
   4. A Fundamental Freedom

II. SEPARATION OF CHURCH AND STATE
   1. The Meaning
   2. The Problem
   3. The Areas of Authority of Each

III. PUBLIC LAW AND THE CHURCH
   1. Churches Subject to Public Law
   2. Vesting of Legal Authority Required
   3. Incorporation and Legal Authority

6

A Free Church in a Free State

A STATEMENT adopted by the Southern Baptist Convention
in 1963 on the Baptist faith and message contains a concise
statement on religious liberty and the separation of church
and state:

God alone is Lord of the conscience, and He has left it free
from the doctrines and commandments of men which are contrary to His Word or not contained in it. Church and state
should be separate. The state owes to the church protection
and full freedom in the pursuit of its spiritual ends. In providing for such freedom no ecclesiastical group or denomination
should be favored by the state more than others. Civil government being ordained of God, it is the duty of Christians to
render loyal obedience thereto in all things not contrary to the
revealed will of God. The church should not resort to the civil
power to carry on its work. The gospel of Christ contemplates
spiritual means alone for the pursuit of its ends. The state has
no right to impose penalties for religious opinions of any kind.
The state has no right to impose taxes for the support of any
form of religion. A free church in a free state is the Christian
ideal, and this implies the right of free and unhindered access
to God on the part of all men, and the right to form and propa-
gate opinions in the sphere of religion without interference by
the civil power.

I. RELIGIOUS LIBERTY

These same beliefs were held by Baptist forefathers
and impelled them to take the lead in making sure that
there would be religious freedom in the United States.
They were largely responsible for the religious liberty
and separation of church and state provided under the

government of the United States. They believed then, as now, in a free church and a free state in a free society.

1. A Basic Principle

Religious liberty means the freedom of choice and the freedom from compulsion in all matters pertaining to one's religious beliefs, practices, and observances. Religious liberty demands equality of religious rights for all persons. It recognizes the right of all men to their own religious or nonreligious convictions without any human imposition. As long as an individual's worship habits, beliefs, or religious practices do not infringe upon the rights of another, he is to be held accountable only to God.

2. A Gift from God

The principle of religious liberty did not originate with man but with God. God made man in his own image and endowed him with the ability and freedom of choice. Man is free to obey or disobey, to acknowledge God as sovereign Lord, or to deny his existence. The only limitation God placed upon this freedom is the warning that man is accountable for the decisions he makes.

History records that what God has so freely given, man has tried to take away. A listing of religious coercions and persecutions would fill volumes. Tyrants in both church and state have denied religious freedom to certain groups of people. Even today religious freedom is lacking in countries controlled by the Roman Catholic hierarchy and in the Communist dominated countries.

People living in the United States today do not realize how great is their heritage of religious liberty. But their forefathers knew what it was like to live in countries where there was no religious liberty. Some men came to America with limited and narrow concepts of religious liberty. But gradually the concepts of religious liberty were expanded to where Thomas Jefferson could say: "No man shall be compelled to frequent or support any religious worship or ministry or shall otherwise suffer on account of his religious opinions or beliefs, but all men shall be free to profess, and by argument to maintain their opinion in matters of religion."

And Abraham Lincoln said: "Fourscore and seven years ago our fathers brought forth on this continent a new nation, conceived in liberty and dedicated to the proposition that all men are created equal."

3. A Legal Provision of Government

Although religious liberty originated in the mind and heart of God, antedates all forms of government, and is an inherent right, its existence in practice demands provision and protection by civil authority.

In spite of the fact that one of the primary purposes of settlers coming to the colonies was to escape religious persecution, complete religious liberty was not practiced among them. Those of different beliefs were refused settlement, banished, or simply tolerated.

Equality of religious rights and privileges did not exist until Roger Williams settled in Rhode Island. He established a democracy in the colony at Providence with majority rule in civil government. One of the chief provisions of this early democratic government was liberty of conscience and practice in religion.

From this significant beginning came the principles of both political democracy and religious liberty which were later written into the Constitution of the United States and the Bill of Rights.

The First Amendment to the Constitution declares that "Congress shall make no law respecting an establishment of religion, or prohibiting the free exercise thereof; or abridging the freedom of speech, or of the press, or the right of the people peaceably to assemble, and to petition the Government for a redress of grievances." A clear and far-reaching interpretation of this amendment was made by the United States Supreme Court in the case of *Everson* vs. *Board of Education*. The following is an excerpt from the court's decision: "Neither a state nor the Federal Government can . . . force nor influence a person to go to or remain away from church against his will or force him to profess a belief or disbelief in any religion. No person can be punished for entertaining or professing religious beliefs or disbeliefs, for church attendance or non-attendance."

The First Amendment acknowledges the inalienable right to religious liberty of all persons and legally guarantees that it shall be both provided and protected.

4. *A Fundamental Freedom*

There are three categories of freedoms which are fundamental to the full and free expression of religious liberty. These may be classified as "freedom of," "freedom to," and "freedom from."

The "freedom of" category includes freedom of beliefs, freedom of worship, and freedom of association. Each individual is to be free at all times to believe or not to believe or to change his beliefs. No one is to force his beliefs on another or to persecute him for what he may believe.

This applies also to worship—private and public. Worship is considered to be man's most sacred freedom, and it must not be infringed upon or violated in any way. The practice of one's beliefs and participation in worship are incomplete without association. While one may manifest his beliefs and worship alone, his freedom is incomplete unless he can do so in the company of others. Therefore, he must possess the freedom of association in private or public gatherings.

"Freedom to" includes the freedom to practice one's religion, to accept or to reject religious teachings, to disseminate religious beliefs, and to participate in religious activities. The only limitation to these freedoms is in recognizing the freedom and rights of others and in maintaining the morality, public order, and the general welfare of a democratic society.

The "freedom from" category includes the freedom from interferences or coercion in religious beliefs, practices, or participation, and the freedom from discrimination because of one's religious beliefs, practices, or participation. Public authorities should never interfere or use force in matters of religion. They should not give preference to one religion or religious body. Instead, they must protect an individual or group of individuals from discrimination by others. Equality before the law is essential to the maintenance of religious liberty. Absolute separation of church and state is the only way there can be equality before the law.

II. SEPARATION OF CHURCH AND STATE

Just as Baptists repudiate all forms of ecclesiastical control and interference, they also repudiate any state control or interference. They believe that a church must be completely free and separate from the state if it is to be true to Christ. There must be no restrictions upon its liberty of thought and action, for only in a free church is the Holy Spirit free to direct. A church must be free and separate from the state, for only then can its members enjoy soul liberty. Any restrictions placed upon a church restricts the religious liberty of its members.

This does not mean that civil laws are to be ignored. Baptists believe that civil authority is of God and is to be obeyed. It is in matters of faith and religious activity that they deny that the state has any jurisidiction.

1. *The Meaning*

C. Emanuel Carlson, executive director of the Baptist Joint Committee on Public Affairs, has written a six-point definition of what Baptists mean by separation of church and state. His definition appeared in *Report from the Capitol,* January, 1959.

DISTINCT "REASONS FOR BEING"

1. Separation means that the church has its own "reasons for being" and that these reasons are distinct from those of the state. Both church and state may desire law and order, defense against foreign enemies, an orderly and just economy, the protection of the person, etc., but these are basically functions of the state and not of the churches. The New Testament presents a church that deals in the gospel, in a fellowship of faith, and in love to all mankind. Its members go out to participate as nobler citizens, but the institutions still have separate raison d'etre.

EACH HAS ITS OWN "PUBLIC"

2. Separation also means that each has its own "public." A person is born into the state, and the political community therefore normally includes all the people. Not all, however, accept the gospel, cultivate Christian faith, or seek to nurture the distinctive Christian way of life. The two "publics" overlap, and the churches should strive to win all. Nonetheless, the two publics are and must be "separate." If the church is a fellowship of faith it must of necessity be a voluntary group.

METHODS MUST BE DIFFERENT

3. Furthermore, the methods of the church must be distinct from those of the state. Military action, police methods, and tax powers are all appropriate and usable toward the objectives of the state. These do not work as means by which to reach spiritual objectives. In contrast, the churches must rely on instruction, worship, prayer, love, to the end that their members may "put on the whole armor of God," including truth, righteousness, peace, faith, the Word, and the many other spiritual graces.

SEPARATE ADMINISTRATION REQUIRED

4. Separation in the above matters requires that there be separate administrations of the two institutions. The church cannot be a "department of ecclesiastical affairs" in the government, and the government cannot be the "action department" of the church. History is replete with evidence that the "use of the churches" for the "moral and spiritual" purposes of government makes them something less than the church of which Christ is Lord. Likewise, when the churches try to reach their objectives by political action, they still have not done their job.

SEPARATE SOURCES OF SUPPORT

5. It follows that the two must have their own separate sources of revenue. The control of the purse presents final control of policy in the life of institutions. Accordingly, institutions that depend on tax funds are basically dependent on government regardless of how the Boards may be chosen. And further, payment of one's taxes involves an experience which is not even similar to Christian stewardship. The qualities of character which are developed by voluntary stewardship cannot be mistaken for those nurtured by the tax collector.

SEPARATE EDUCATIONAL PROGRAMS

6. If the above distinctions are valid, it also follows that church and state must each have their own appropriate educational programs. The churches cannot delegate the education of their members and of their leaders to the state. Neither is it in order for the churches to attempt to monopolize the channels of knowledge so as to limit the political and economic order to the scope of the church programs. The former arrangement has always paralyzed the church and the latter arrangement has stagnated the state.

2. *The Problem*

Attention is being focused on the mounting problem of church and state relationships. Both the denominational and secular presses have had much to report on the subject. Both church and government leaders have debated the issue. Confusion prevails in the minds of many people because of the complexity of the problem and the absence of clear-cut solutions.

For example, within the space of weeks, presidents and deans of Southern Baptist colleges voted to back Federal loans to education. The Executive Board of the Texas Baptist General Convention voted just the opposite. In their annual conventions some states voted to accept Federal funds; others rejected them.

In conferences conducted by eight Baptist groups in Illinois in the spring of 1961, a number of problems related to the separation of church and state were discussed. A partial list of these problems reveals the growing complexity of the church-state issue. Included were aids to education, public health, welfare services, civil defense, censorship, blue laws, religion in public schools, the church and tax policies, purchase of churches by the state as historic shrines, zoning problems involving the location of new churches, and problems involving churches and their institutions in redevelopment areas.

What does all of this have to do with Baptist polity and government? Simply this: Federal grants and loans always have strings attached. Certain rules and specifications must be met. When a church or denominational institution accepts funds and agrees to these rules and specifications, it ceases to be completely autonomous.

The state is to be just as free and separate from the church as the church is free and separate from the state. Baptists accept this as just and right. They do not want the state to meddle in church or denominational affairs, and they believe that a church or denomination should not meddle in state affairs. This does not mean that a church is not to preach and teach and encourage individual action on the part of its members. Neither does it mean that a convention should not vote a resolution directed against some state legislative or executive action. It does mean, however, that a church or denomination as a body is not to attempt to force the state to conform to what it believes to be right and desirable.

In a democracy individuals can best enjoy the freedoms and the equal rights and privileges ordained of God for man. History has proved that only in democratic countries can there be absolute separation of church and state. While Baptists believe this, they do not think it is a church's business to coerce or conscript its members in any collective effort to bring about changes in government. To do so would be a violation of the principle of individual freedom of choice and action as well as the principle of separation of church and state.

3. The Areas of Authority of Each

When a church is involved in conducting public worship, observing the ordinances, preaching the gospel, and teaching its doctrines, the state acknowledges it to be an entity owing allegiance only to its spiritual superior. For Baptists, this is the Lord. The state also acknowledges the freedom of a church to determine the nature of its government, to regulate its membership, to choose its leaders, and to carry on missionary work at home and abroad. These are all considered to be within the authority of the church, and the state recognizes that, constitutionally, it has no right to interfere.

When a church buys property, builds buildings, provides parking, conducts street services or parades, and in other ways conducts its business or extends its ministries into the community, it enters areas where the state has authority. At least two court decisions illustrate this division of authority.

In Colorado, the State Supreme Court in dismissing a dispute between factions of a church ruled that "civil courts have no authority to inquire into ecclesiastical questions of an independent congregation." The key to this decision is primarily in the words "ecclesiastical question" and secondarily in the words "independent congregation."

By majority vote the church had made its decision, and the minority was seeking a court injunction to prevent the church from doing what it had voted to do. The court recognized that in "independent congregations" decisions are made by majority vote and therefore no individual rights had been violated. Even more important, it recognized that it had no authority to intervene in the governmental affairs of a church.

In Kentucky, the Court of Appeals ruled that minors have a right to vote in a Baptist church because it is "the established rule or custom of the church." The church had voted to buy property, but a minority group had contested it on the basis that if minors had not been permitted to vote the proposal to buy the property would have failed.

Why did the court hear and rule on the second case and not the first? Because the question of purchase and ownership of property was involved, and this comes under the domain of public law.

III. PUBLIC LAW AND THE CHURCH

Although public laws vary from state to state, the following generally prevails as applied to churches and other religious bodies. The state looks upon the church as being both a spiritual body and a temporal body. As a spiritual body the church is separate and apart from the state. It is considered to be a spiritual body and under no authority of the state when it is engaged in its spiritual functions.

When a church conducts its business in the community, it becomes a temporal body in the eyes of the state and thereby becomes subject to public law. Churches may conduct their spiritual ministries and carry on their business affairs without being aware of the difference. Under public law, however, there is a distinct difference. The state clearly distinguishes between the spiritual and the temporal functions of religious bodies.

1. Churches Subject to Public Law

Christ commanded his followers to "render therefore unto Caesar the things which are Caesar's" (Matt. 22:21). The Holy Spirit led Peter to write, "Submit yourselves to every ordinance of man for the Lord's sake" (1 Peter 2:13). Although these teachings were directed primarily to individual Christians, they apply equally well to congregations. Only when the laws of state are in opposition to the laws of God are Christians justified in rejecting them.

A church's decision or practice that runs counter to public law is held by the state to be invalid. For example, the government does not tax real estate used by churches in their spiritual ministries, but if a church acquires and uses property in the operation of a business, the property is subject to taxation.

A church cannot violate the peace, morality, safety, or good order of a community and claim freedom of religion even though these are rightfully considered as spiritual functions. A church is not permitted by the state to exercise its rights when it violates the rights of its citizens and vice versa.

The woman pastor of a religious sect was fined when she defied a court order to stop disturbing the peace in the neighborhood of her home. She said in defense, "I have to do what God tells me to do, regardless." She also claimed that the court's injunction was in violation of the constitutional provision for freedom of worship. In his ruling the judge said to the woman: "No one is denying you the right to worship as you see fit, but you cannot disturb your neighbors. That is a violation of the law."

While church business and activity in a community must conform to public law, public law must conform to the United States Constitution. The Fourteenth Amendment guarantees that "no state shall make or enforce any law which shall abridge the privileges or immunities of citizens of the United States; nor shall any state deprive any person of life, liberty, or property without due process of law; nor deny any person within its jurisdiction the equal protection of the laws."

The First Amendment guarantees privileges and immunities that state civil laws cannot abridge. If a church feels that its rights have been breached, it has access to due process of law. However, it is never desirable for a church to seek court actions if it is possible to settle the case out of court.

2. Vesting of Legal Authority Required

States refuse to do business directly with voluntary societies. Too many people are involved and memberships are too fluid. Courts have held that legal suits cannot be filed by or against voluntary societies. Therefore, voluntary societies must either vest title and trust of property in a small group of trustees or become a chartered corporation. Most states have provisions permitting the incorporation of churches.

The church as a temporal body is looked upon as a voluntary society if unincorporated, and as a corporation if incorporated. A society is considered by the state to be the congregation assembled for the purpose of administering its business affairs. Yet it is limited in that it cannot enter into civil contracts or acquire, manage, or dispose of real property in its own name.

A church may have its officers, committees, and regular meetings, operate under a constitution, and hold chattel property. But if it comes into possession of real property, the state requires that the legal title be vested in the name of trustees. When this is done, the control of the property passes from the society to the trustees, with the society retaining the beneficiary rights.

Once elected, a trustee cannot be removed by the church, without the approval of the state through its courts. A successor must be appointed in the same way.

An unincorporated society cannot contract or be contracted with. It cannot sue or be sued or compromise a suit. The trustees are vested with the authority to act on behalf of the church.

Trustees of unincorporated societies have been known to prevent the sale of property, refuse to mortgage the property in order for churches to secure loans, and to block the expansion and growth of churches in general. Churches have frequently become involved in time- and money-consuming court procedures in order to quiet title to property signed by trustees no longer living or by those refusing to carry out the instructions of a church.

As long as trustees co-operate in carrying out the will of the congregation, as the law requires them to do, an unincorporated society may get along reasonably well. But the surest safeguard to congregational polity is to place no legal authority in the hands of any group or individual. The best way to insure congregational control is for the church to become a membership corporation.

3. *Incorporation and Legal Authority*

There are three types or methods of incorporation—corporation sole, trustee corporation, and membership corporation. Corporation sole is for those bodies, notably Catholics, whose polity prohibits lay participation in legal affairs, and whose authority and title to property is vested in a priest or ruling bishop.

In a trustee corporation, specific persons or officers are authorized to act as trustees for the incorporated body. The society elects the trustees of the corporation and the control of the property and legal affairs passes to them. They alone may make contracts and manage the realty. As long as they properly exercise their trust, they are not responsible to the society as far as the state is concerned.

The difference between the trustee corporation and the unincorporated society is that under the former a church or convention retains both the title and the beneficial interests. This means that the members and not the trustees have the authority in mortgaging or selling the property. They also have the right to perpetual succession (the right to elect, replace, or fill a vacancy without court action) of the trustees. Only the members can consider amendments to the articles of incorporation. It will be readily recognized that this type of incorporation is better suited to convention agencies and to churches that practice presbyterian polity.

It is only in the membership corporation that congregational polity can be fully practiced. A membership corporation is similar to a civil or business corporation with church members corresponding to directors. Officers of a membership corporation hold no trust and function only as administrative officials, always subordinate to the congregation met in business session. The congregation not only possesses the beneficial interests but is also in absolute control. A membership corporation usually is granted at least the following powers by the state:

It may determine the qualifications of its members and admit and withdraw fellowship from whom it will.

It may conduct elections without interference, elect such officers as it deems necessary, and remove from office and fill any vacancies.

It may enjoy perpetual succession of its corporate officers, changing officers and filling vacancies when and as often as it pleases.

It may receive and dispose of money, property, (real, personal, or mixed), whether by gift, devise, bequest, or purchase.

It may borrow and repay money in its corporate name rather than in the name of trustees or other individuals.

It may hold money and property in trust for individuals or other bodies provided that the purpose of the trust is not hostile to its own.

It may sue, be sued, or compromise suits in its corporate name.

It may enter into contracts as a recognized and responsible institution duly chartered by the state.

It may establish branch Sunday schools, mission stations, and assist in the organization of new churches in its corporate name.

It may adopt necessary bylaws, policies, and rules and regulations to manage its corporate affairs, as long as these are in harmony with its charter and not inconsistent with the laws of the state.

These or similar powers are available to any Baptist church within a state where they are provided if it will take the necessary steps to become an incorporated church.

Frequently, attention is not given to the corporate status of a church when all is serene in the life of a congregation. All too often it is only when confronted with a difficult legal problem that a church may realize what it has forfeited in not becoming incorporated. This need not happen. A little forethought, planning, and effort will provide a church with the status and powers granted to it by a state through incorporation.

CHAPTER 7

7

Dangerous Drifts in Baptist Government

BAPTIST GOVERNMENT is often in danger of drifting into practices which are contrary to congregational polity. These practices sometimes begin when a church or denominational body finds it necessary to assign work to an increasing number of individuals or groups. In other instances drifts may occur when one or a few individuals begin to feel that only they are able to make decisions in a Baptist body. Or a church or denominational body may simply drift into undemocratic practices through ignorance or indifference. Whenever or however a drift begins, it is usually imperceptible. It is always away from democracy with more powers being exercised by individuals and less by the people as a whole.

These movements away from democracy are purposely called "drifts." While they may be definite enough to be evident, few who are carried along in them are aware that they exist. This lack of awareness makes them all the more dangerous. Should they be permitted to continue, they will tend to grow deep and strong; and it becomes increasingly difficult to return to democratic practices.

In addition to calling these movements drifts, they are purposely designated an "ism." This is done deliberately with the hope that Baptists will be alerted to the incompatibility of these drifts in their government with true Baptist polity.

I. LIBERALISM

Liberalism is defined by Wayne E. Ward and W. Boyd Hunt in an article in the *Encyclopedia of Southern Baptists*: "In recent years the term 'liberalism' has become a theological title intended to characterize a thinker of unorthodox bent who emphasizes free-thinking with regard to the classical doctrinal statements of the Christian faith. Such thinking is usually marked by philosophical and religious idealism, a rejection of the authority of the Scriptures in Christian faith and practice, . . . an emphasis on the role of Christ as ethical teacher rather than as divine Redeemer and Lord" (786).

Baptist polity is an outgrowth of New Testament doctrines. When there is a compromise of these basic doctrines, a compromise in polity developed from these doctrines invariably follows. Likewise, a compromise in polity leads to further compromises in doctrine. Evidence is that the two are inseparable. What affects one affects the other.

Individuals who reject the Bible as the divine and inerrant word of God naturally do not hold to the polity built upon New Testament principles. Some, however, profess to accept the inerrancy of the Scriptures, yet at the same time manifest liberal views toward polity.

The drift of liberalism in polity leads to the building of polity on the principle of expediency rather than on the New Testament principles. It leads to the belief that polity should be fluid and easily adaptable to changing needs and to new situations. Ultimately, it calls for polity to have sufficient elasticity to meet any demands that current conditions make of it.

In the drift of liberalism in polity, it is advocated that each generation work out its own polity in keeping with its needs and desires of its own day. If the drift is permitted to continue, polity will be constantly changing.

II. RITUALISM

Ritualism in churches does not always pertain to ceremonial worship or religious rites. A drift into ritualistic practices in church government may occur. This happens when procedures become so habitual that they are rigidly followed and people perfunctorily go through the motions of being democratic.

Receiving new members into the church fellowship is one of the most obvious rituals into which a church may drift. The ritual is performed when new people unite with the church. The members unthinkingly go through the established ritual of raising one hand while buttoning coats, reaching for Bibles, and making other preparation to leave as quickly as possible.

The ritual of approval is another practice to be avoided. It is performed in the business meetings of churches when the members indifferently vote their approval of reports to which they pay no attention and to recommendations about which they have little knowledge or concern.

The ritual of approval reaches an extreme when it is not considered necessary to take the negative vote on a question. In the automatic raising of hands in quick approval of whatever is presented, it is assumed that everyone is for it and that taking the opposite vote is not necessary. This should never happen in a Baptist church. Even if only one person wishes to declare his convictions by casting his vote in opposition, he should be given the privilege of doing so. Not to afford him this opportunity is to give lip service to the principle of equal rights and privileges in church government.

It is not in churches alone that reports and recommendations are frequently approved in ritualistic fashion. Sometimes in an annual convention a moderator can hear a motion, get a second, rap his gavel, and declare it passed without a majority of the people knowing what issue is being voted on. The disconcerting thing about such a performance is that the people enjoy and encourage it. They approve of dispensing with the business of a convention so that they can proceed with more enjoyable things, such as visiting with friends in the corridors.

Another ritual Baptists should avoid drifting into is the custom of committees in churches and denominational bodies presenting recommendations which are already cut and dried. This happens when committee members think that they must come to a decision on a matter before presenting it to the congregation. They weigh the pros and cons, make the decision, and recommend that a vote of approval be given to what they have already decided should be done. Then hands go up as the congregation participates in its ritual of approval.

Ritualism can become deeply ingrained in the governmental practices in churches and denominational bodies. The drift becomes apparent when someone attempts to disturb the ritual.

III. TRADITIONALISM

Closely akin to the drift of ritualism is the drift of traditionalism. In some instances this drift is a result of combating liberal views and practices, while in others it is simply a result of being satisfied and comfortable with the status quo. This drift reaches its ultimate danger when traditional ways of doing things become so firmly established that members equate them with doctrines.

Many new pastors have been confronted with the statement, "We don't do it that way in our church." Some churches still do not have budgets because they have gotten along for many years without a budget. All business matters in some churches are considered to be the prerogative of the deacons rather than of the congregation because of long-established practice.

In a meeting of leaders in one church there was a frank facing of the problem of too many major emphases in the fall months. Someone proposed as a solution the moving of the budget campaign to the early spring. Immediately there was strong resistance—the resistance of traditionalism. It was instanteous and without careful consideration and evaluation of the proposal. The church had always had its campaign in the fall, and it believed that the campaign would not be successful if conducted at any other date.

It is traditional in some churches to elect deacons "for life." The same few men hold the position year in and year out whether they actually serve or not. Frequently they are a self-perpetuating body inasmuch as they control the election of new deacons. Often they control it to the extent that they never see the need of new men. In some churches, few, if any, of the members have a choice in the selections of deacons. They are forced to follow leaders whom they had no voice in electing. This is neither democratic nor right. They are the victims of traditionalism.

A pastor told of a problem he was having in the handling of finances in the church he had been serving only a few weeks. For over twenty years the treasurer of this church had gathered the offerings, carried them home, and counted them. On Monday morning he deposited the money in a bank account on which only he could write checks. He exercised almost absolute control of purchases and never made a financial report to the congregation, except to tell how much was in the account if asked. This church had drifted into this traditional way of handling its finances and in doing so had surrendered its right to receive, handle, and disburse its funds.

To avoid such undemocratic practices a church would do well to adopt the procedure for handling church funds as set forth in the *Church Finance Record System Manual* by Crowe and Moore. If followed, this procedure will safeguard the church's democracy in the area of controlling its financial affairs.

Writing on "The Place of Tradition," Editor C. R. Daley said:

> To accept tradition without careful consideration is unwise. It leads to closed minds, dogmatism and sterility. . . .
>
> Much in the popular Baptist belief and polity of our day is tradition and should be recognized as such. . . .
>
> More than in what we believe we are traditionists in how we do things. This is all right until the tradition becomes regarded as the only proper way and all other ways are wrong. For example, there is a tradition about how to constitute a Baptist church, how to ordain deacons or a gospel preacher. The tradition varies slightly from place to place, but any variance from the traditional way is looked upon as wrong. It might well be that there is a much better way than the traditional way. . . .
>
> Let's learn how to use tradition. Let's conserve from it what serves our need, but not hold to all of it until it makes mummies of us.[1]

The safe practice is periodically to analyze the methods and procedures used in church government and to evaluate them in the light of the New Testament principles of Baptist polity. While in some instances it may be in order to do things in a traditional manner, Baptists should act on principle rather than tradition.

IV. OFFICIALISM

The concern of officialism here is not so much with church or denominational "officials" as it is with the strict

---

[1] Quoted in *The Baptist Messenger*, L (July 6, 1961), 16.

adherence to the methods, procedures, plans, requirements, and the like which these leaders promote and with which they are identified. Baptists sometimes drift into the habit of considering something official if it is in a manual or printed in a periodical or originates in a convention office. They drift into the pattern of thinking a statement is official if the pastor, the chairman of deacons, or a committee chairman said it.

Some people have become so accustomed to official regulations, forms, and routines in their businesses or places of employment that they have come to expect the same in their church and denomination. It is important to them that what is said or written pertaining to their participation in church activities come from those in the top echelon of authority. They want to be told what pattern to follow, and in the absence of a set pattern for doing things, they are prone to be confused and stymied. Officialism provides them with a sense of security, and they are easily caught up in the drift.

Perhaps the drift of officialism is partly the result of a desire on the part of some to be loyal followers of their leaders. But to question or object to a proposal does not mean disloyalty nor does it show disrespect for those who proposed it. One can question or voice disagreement without being contentious or dogmatic. If because of a conviction one raises a question or takes an opposing view, he may render a real service to his church or denomination.

Officialism is full of pressures to conform. It is also full of administrative rules. Schedules, forms, and reports must all be uniform. Work must be done in a set manner. Rules, schedules, forms, and reports are all necessary, but they must never become more important than the people for whom they are made.

In a Baptist church the ruled are the rulers. When what a leader or a manual says becomes more important than what the Bible says about the priesthood of a believer or the autonomy of a church, then the drift of officialism has become deep and dangerous.

V. CENTRALISM

Churches and denominational bodies have not escaped the influence of business and industry toward greater centralization. While centralization makes for better control and perhaps increased efficiency, it has inherent dangers for Baptist democracy. Organizational charts of churches, associations, conventions and their agencies are excellent aids if properly understood and used. If not, they can contribute significantly to the drift of centralism. Baptists face the danger more today than ever before of centering more and more powers in deacons and committees, in church staffs, in denominational boards, and in executive secretaries.

An example of the drift toward centralism is the action taken in some few churches which adopt the policy that all committee chairmen must be deacons. In this arrangement, the deacons approximate a board of control such as is found in large secular organizations.

A strong emphasis on administrative efficiency has been a major contributor to this drift. More and more functions which once were considered governmental are now considered administrative. The drift of centralism sets in when these functions are transferred from the people to the administrators. In the churches, the transference may be made to pastors and employed staffs. In the conventions, it may be made to executive or agency boards. These boards in turn may grant the sanctions of government to the administrator.

When there is a drift of centralism, where does the fault lie? In the pastor or denominational executive? Not necessarily. In the deacons or denominational boards?

Partly. In the members of congregations or messengers to the conventions? Largely. The people are simply carried along in the drift. They find it much easier to leave everything in the hands of their leaders and boards.

To avoid this dangerous drift of centralism, Baptists would do well to heed the warning of E. S. James:

Not long ago the masses participated in all decisions about Baptist business and endeavors. Today there is a strong trend to leave most everything to committees and boards. This is an exceedingly dangerous move. Few would believe it could ever lead to a Baptist episcopacy or hierarchy, but few Christians in the second century would have dreamed of such a thing as the papacy.

Such things don't happen overnight. They result from a long period of delegated authority, and the only assurance against them is for all the people to know all about all the work and have a voice in all the decisions.[2]

VI. AUTHORITARIANISM

The term authoritarianism as applied to church government denotes the surrender of individual freedom of judgment and action and submitting to the power and influence of those in positions of leadership. Authoritarianism both grows out of and contributes to centralism. One is the natural result of the other.

It seems that it is rather easy for authoritarian groups to develop in supposedly democratic churches. Deacons are sometimes called "boards" with no action considered to be official unless they originate or approve it. Finance committees have been known to gain such control of the finances as to be able to refuse to act in accordance with the vote of a congregation. Pastor and other staff leaders in some instances have become so authoritarian in their administrative practices as habitually to make decisions

[2] *The Baptist Standard,* as quoted in *The Baptist Messenger,* L (December 7, 1961), 3.

and take action without securing the approval of the members of the church.

When more and more of the functions of government are placed in the hands of boards, committees, and employed administrators, there is danger that authoritarianism will develop. It happens when individuals or committees assume power needed to carry out their responsibilities. The drift is in evidence when these individuals or small groups of individuals begin to make decisions and determine policies for the people. The ultimate result is that instead of government by the people—a democracy—there is government by the few—an oligarchy.

Authoritarianism may drift to an even greater extreme. Instead of government being in the hands of a few, one person may gain such ascendancy and power as to control all decisions and action affecting a congregation or denominational agency. When this happens, democracy has changed into a monarchy.

VII. PROTECTIONISM

Usually, protectionism arises in a church or denominational body from the best of motives: the strong wish to protect the weak; the informed, the ignorant; and the sophisticated, the innocent. However good the motive, protectionism denies soul competency of the individual and equality to all members.

Perhaps protectionism is practiced more in the area of suppression of information than in any other area. Admonitions to deacons, committee members, and organizational heads not to discuss certain matters with the people contribute to this drift. The idea is that it is better for the people to continue in ignorance than to be disturbed with the problems with which the smaller group is concerned.

Frequently, the thought behind protecting the people

from knowing is a desire to maintain a high degree of morale. For example, a budget committee does not disclose specific items and amounts in the budget, but lumps them together in general categories. It is feared that some items may be misunderstood and objected to by some of the people. These objections are to be avoided because they might adversely affect the morale of the people. The morale must be protected if at all possible, even at the cost of democracy.

Protectionism usually causes any opposition to become taboo. If a member opposes a recommendation, his opposition is frowned upon by leaders and members alike. They do not wish anyone to disturb the status quo, and there is a rush to protect it when it is in danger. Members get to the place where they prefer to go blindly on, indifferently approving any recommendation or action already taken. They do not wish to be suspected of being disloyal or uncooperative by asking questions or voicing opposition.

T. B. Maston made some important observations in an article "Criticism and Comment." He warned against the suppression of criticism and the growing disinclination of Baptists to speak out concerning denominational affairs. In it he says:

There may be some areas of our denominational life where rather tragic mistakes are being made simply because not enough people will speak out. How can we improve our methods, how can we gain new insights into the truth unless channels of communication and discussion are kept open? How can wise decisions be made concerning some trends and developments within our denomination unless varying viewpoints are openly expressed? Some way we need to create the atmosphere that will make it possible for us to differ and yet respect one another.[3]

---

[3] *The Baptist Messenger*, L (October 19, 1961), 3 ff.

Avoiding debate in Baptist conventions is a good example of the reluctance of individuals to speak out. Moderators aware of this sentiment have found an easy way to protect the people (and themselves) from argumentative outbursts. They simply entertain a motion to refer the matter to a committee. Usually there is quick action from the floor in that direction. Then the decision reached by the few members of the committee becomes the decision of the body when the report is made, and the ritual of approval is performed. Debate and argument on the floor have been avoided, but democratic rule has been forfeited.

The number of protectors of the people seems to be rapidly increasing in churches and denominational bodies. The number of Baptists who desire to be protected is also increasing. It seems relatively easy for church and denominational leaders as well as Baptists in general to be caught up in the drift of protectionism.

VIII. FEDERALISM

Federalism is the principle of government whereby otherwise autonomous bodies subordinate their authority in affairs common to all to a higher authority. It is expedient that churches and denominational bodies work together in certain types of mission work for example. But great care must be exercised by the leaders of all bodies concerned that this lack of caution may not result in federalism.

In a plan providing loans to churches, the church requesting the loan, the association, the state convention, and an agency of the Southern Baptist Convention are all involved. At least the structure of federalism may be seen in the church's dependence on the endorsement of the association, of both the church's and association's dependence upon the approval of the state convention, and of final approval and granting of the loan by the Southern Baptist Convention agency. In this type of joint participation there is always the danger of the subordination of autonomy, at least to some degree, to the next largest body. If this should occur, federalism becomes active.

Salary supplements of pastors is another dangerous area where the drift of federalism may set in. The church requests it, the association approves it, and the state convention and the Convention agency approve and grant it. There is also a growing practice of making salary supplements to denominational leaders in the states and in the associations.

Baptists reject government grants and loans on the principle of separation of church and state. The principle of separate and independent, autonomous bodies in our Baptist denomination should cause some serious thinking concerning the continuance of these salary supplements.

Richard Carlton, an area missionary in Ohio, wrote an article in which he dealt with the question of responsibility in starting missions. He wrote: "Baptists believe that missions be church-sponsored! Yet, some churches are succumbing, maybe unconsciously, to the idea that the primary role in starting missions belongs to the missionary. Subsequently, the church assumes a subordinate role to that of the missionary; ie., the church helps the missionary to start missions." [4]

Is not the attitude reflected in this complaint the result of an increased tendency of subordination by churches to a denominational body?

The danger of the federalism drift is seen in the change that has taken place in associations. Formerly, associations were instruments of the churches. Now they are increasingly becoming instruments of the two larger denomina-

---

[4] "Starting Missions—Whose Responsibility?," *The Baptist Program* (March, 1960), p. 33.

tional bodies, particularly the state convention. A study of the program of annual meetings and of programs projected into the churches during the year reflects this change.

In 1961, a state convention adopted standards for ordination proceedings including prerequisites, procedure, and order of service. It will be interesting to observe the implementation of this action in churches and associations. On the surface it would seem that it can result in nothing less than the subordination of authority of churches to the convention. This is what has happened in practice of American Baptists in New Jersey. The New Jersey Baptist Convention voted the requirement "that representatives of the State Convention shall participate in ordination examining councils." The next step could well be for ordination to become a function of the convention and not of the churches. This is the extent to which the drift of federalism could unltimately lead.

IX. Ecclesiasticism

The drift of ecclesiasticism is potentially if not actually intermixed with the other drifts. If these drifts are allowed to begin and to continue on their course, ecclesiasticism will ultimately result. It is the drift toward the super Church—one Southern Baptist Church, whether it is called church or convention, made up of local churches with ascending levels of authority. As early as 1934, W. W. Barnes, long-time professor of church history at Southwestern Baptist Theological Seminary, warned Southern Baptists of the direction toward which they were drifting. In the Introduction of *The Southern Baptist Convention: A Study in the Development of Ecclesiology,* he said: "The term 'Southern Baptist Church' is not quite orthodox, but within another generation or two it may attain wide popularity and perfect ecclesiastical respectability."

To many Baptists this statement may seem to be that of an alarmist. Nevertheless, it is a statement that should evoke serious thought. It is a warning to Southern Baptists of the need to assume greater responsibility for the government in their churches and denominational meetings. Baptists must return to the principles of New Testament polity. They must establish the necessary safeguards that will prevent them from getting caught in these dangerous drifts.

W. W. Barnes' appeal made in 1934 needs to be heeded today.

Let our people return to the emphasis upon the voluntary principle in religious experience and in religious work. Let the Southern Baptist Convention and all the other conventions be considered, not ecclesiastical organizations composed of churches, but voluntary organizations composed of individuals who are affiliated together for a common missionary task. Let us forsake the *presbygationalism* that infests us from the local church through organized life into the Southern Baptist Convention and return to the congregational government that is yet our theory.[5]

---

[5] *The Southern Baptist Convention: A Study in the Development of Ecclesiology* (Fort Worth: By the author, 1934), p. 78.

CHAPTER 8

I. LEADERS COMMITTED TO THE DEMOCRATIC IDEAL

    1. New Testament Principles Practiced

    2. Democracy Maintained

    3. Administration Subordinated to Government

II. MEMBERS EDUCATED IN DEMOCRATIC FUNDAMENTALS

    1. Understanding Baptist Polity

    2. Informed About Church and Denominational Affairs

    3. Trained in the Art of Self-government

III. SAFEGUARDS PROVIDED FOR DEMOCRATIC CONTROL

    1. Constitution and Bylaws

    2. Parliamentary Rules

    3. Church Council

IV. DECISIONS REACHED THROUGH DEMOCRATIC ACTION

    1. Business Meetings Well Attended

    2. Motions Thoroughly Discussed

    3. Voting Taken Seriously

8

Maintaining a True Democracy

The tendency for churches and denominational bodies to drift away from the practice of Baptist polity in government demonstrates the need for vigilance in maintaining New Testament principles. This is not easy, for the governed are themselves those who govern.

A true democracy depends upon the active and continuous consent of the people. It also depends upon the principle of voluntariness. Herein lies both the problem and the solution, The problem arises when a voluntary people become lax and indifferent toward the principles of self-government.

Members do not bother to inform themselves. They stay away from business meetings. If they are present when business is transacted, they do not enter into discussions. They either vote absent-mindedly or not at all. Eventually the people do not govern themselves; they leave their government in the hands of the few. The solution is (1) leaders committed to the democratic ideal; (2) members educated in democratic fundamentals; (3) safeguards provided for democratic control; and (4) decisions reached through democratic action.

I. Leaders Committed to the Democratic Ideal

The extent to which the people truly govern themselves in a church or denominational body largely depends upon those who hold offices in the governmental structure. The pastor, other staff members, deacons, church officers, committee chairmen, and organizational heads must believe so strongly in congregational government that they will make no decision or take any action that will do violence to the democratic ideal. This must also be true as far as possible of denominational leaders.

1. *New Testament Principles Practiced*

To believe, teach, and preach the New Testament principles of polity is one thing; to practice them is another. But they must be practiced if democracy is to prevail. Leaders must bear personal witness to the existence of these principles by their deeds. They cannot give assent to congregational polity while governing in such a manner as to violate these principles. They must live up to the polity they proclaim. If they do not, the principles will degenerate into little more than hazy generalities, and the people will develop an apathetic attitude toward personal democratic responsibility.

2. *Democracy Maintained*

A good leader wants to be efficient. He wants to make progress, to achieve a high degree of quality in his work, and to do it in the minimum amount of time. Within the framework of a democracy this can be a frustrating experience. A government operating on congregational polity is the slowest type of government in its functions. The interval of time between the business meetings of a church and referrals to committees for study can mean days and sometimes weeks of delay. Faced with these delays, a leader anxious to complete an assignment is tempted to take action without first securing majority consent.

Those who lead in a church are to conduct themselves as servants of the church. A servant does not issue the orders; he obeys them. So must be the relation of leader to people in a democracy. The leader dedicated to following God's Word in church polity will maintain this relationship in church government.

3. *Administration Subordinated to Government*

Today administrative procedures are emphasized, and good administrators are in demand. This is true in denominations as well as in the business world. High on the list of qualifications for church and denominational leaders is proficiency in administration. Frequently we see or hear references to the pastor as the pastor-administrator or the chief administrator. Larger churches are now employing business administrators. Good business administrative procedures are being practiced in an increasing number of churches. Some churches are restructuring their organizational procedures so that the organizations can be better administered.

In good administration there must be delegation. Where there is delegation, there must be controls. Further, centralization of controls must reside in the top administrator. But there is a difference in administrative control and governmental authority. The former must always be kept subordinate to the latter.

Administration is a tool of government and must never become a substitute for it. When it does, the administrator governs as well as administers. Leaders are administrators; but as they administer, they must never permit administrative decisions or procedures to supplant the functions of government.

II. MEMBERS EDUCATED IN DEMOCRATIC FUNDAMENTALS

When individuals become members of a Baptist body, they assume a moral and spiritual obligation to participate actively in its government. In order to do so in an adequate manner they need to understand Baptist polity, to keep informed about church and denominational affairs, and to develop competency in the art of democratic government.

1. *Understanding Baptist Polity*

Polity is an unknown word to some Baptists. They may have read or studied the Scriptures which set forth the principles of polity, but they have never seen them applied to church government. This ignorance has contributed significantly to the dangerous drifts away from the practice of true democracy.

What the Bible teaches about polity must be known and understood before it can be adequately practiced in church government. Howard P. Colson emphasized this need when he wrote: "We like to glory in the fact that our churches and our denomination as a whole represent the New Testament ideal of spiritual democracy. But all students of democracy recognize that the education of the people who make up the democracy is essential to its proper and effective functioning. We can make our Baptist ideal work only in the measure in which our people are biblically taught and trained." [1]

While leaders are responsible for this teaching and training, all members share in the responsibility. It is their duty to read and study and pray so that they can understand the New Testament principles of polity.

2. *Informed About Church and Denominational Affairs*

It has been said that democracy feeds on information and dies without it. Only an informed people can intelligently govern themselves. If leaders withhold information or if the people do not exercise the necessary initiative to keep informed, democracy suffers. Its strength or weak-

---

[1] "Our 1960 'Jubilee' Emphasis," *The Quarterly Review*, XX (First Quarter, 1960), 11.

ness depends to a large degree on the extent of the knowledge of church and denominational affairs of those participating in the business sessions.

Church members need information about what is going on in their church and in their denomination. So does the messenger from the church to a denominational convention. The affairs of a church are intertwined with those of the denomination and those of the denomination with those of its affiliated churches. Thus to participate intelligently in the business session of either, one needs to keep himself informed concerning them.

As churches and denominational bodies grow larger and their business becomes more complex, it becomes increasingly difficult to keep informed. Through church bulletins, newspapers, mail-outs, public announcements in the churches, and through the facilities of the denominational press, information is available.

One church departed from the usual in the mailing of its bulletin. In addition to the regular format a smaller, colored sheet which quickly attracted attention was stapled to it. Printed on this sheet were the recommendations which the deacons would present to the church for consideration at the forthcoming business meeting.

3. *Trained in the Art of Self-government*

Ideally, each Baptist body is self-governing. The degree of success it achieves in self-government depends on the extent of participation by those who make up the body. How well each member functions in the self-governing process is the measure to which the body achieves and maintains a true democracy.

In self-government there must be free discussion. Each person has the right to express himself and should be encouraged to do so. As he participates, he will gain confidence and competency.

When members discuss a matter, differences inevitably arise, and the discussion of these differences is what keeps democracy alive. It is important, however, that these differences never be permitted to become divisive. The love that binds Christians to Christ and to one another must always prevail. Good training will focus attention on this essential in a spiritual democracy.

Good moderators can do much to train members in the art of self-government by the manner in which they encourage the people to speak out. They can also train them in parliamentary procedure and in maintaining a friendly, cordial atmosphere.

When the vote is taken on a matter, those voting with the minority should quickly rally to support the majority decision. The unity of a church is too important for members to do otherwise. A word of caution is in order at this point. Unity must follow free discussion. The desire to maintain unity should never suppress discussion. This denies members' their rights and privileges.

H. H. McGinty asks two pertinent questions of those who might have difficulty in accepting majority decisions: "When will we learn that a Baptist church operates on the principles of a Christian democracy? And when will the members of these churches accept the fact that in a Christian democracy one cannot always have his way?"[2] The member who insists on his own way in a church seeking to maintain a democracy is infringing on the will of the majority. He has not learned the art of self-government.

III. SAFEGUARDS PROVIDED FOR DEMOCRATIC CONTROL

The denominational bodies have provided safeguards which help to maintain control by the people in the an-

---

[2] *Word and Way,* as quoted in *The Baptist Standard,* LXXII (April 20, 1960), 5.

nual meetings and in the boards and agencies between these meetings. These safeguards are such things as articles of incorporation, constitution and bylaws, and rules of parliamentary procedure. Many churches have provided these safeguards, but a majority probably have not.

1. Constitution and Bylaws

Churches are discovering that a constitution and bylaws provide them with legal protection before the law and help them resolve complex problems.

A church constitution may be defined as a written instrument which sets forth the basic principles and regulations by which a church governs itself. Bylaws are the secondary rules which make effective these principles and regulations.

A constitution usually contains such items as name and location, corporate status, purpose, basis of membership, governing procedures, officers, meetings, fiscal policy, organizations, ordinances, licensing and ordaining, basis of co-operation with other Baptist bodies, and provisions for amendments.

The bylaws include qualifications for membership and the removal and disciplining of members; how general church officers are to be elected, their term of office, their duties, and steps for filling a vacancy; the principle functions of each of the church organizations and the leaders of these organizations and their duties; the church committees and their responsibilities; the church council and its responsibilities and meetings; items pertaining to church finance, such as the preparation of the budget, the financial enlistment campaign, policies regarding expenditures, the auditing of records; buildings and equipment, their maintenance and repair, and policies regarding their use; insurance; and other such items. Provision for amending the bylaws is also included.

A constitution and bylaws give a church safeguards to its congregational government in several ways:

(1) They provide a written medium of information about the government of a church.

(2) They help avoid the usurping of authority.

(3) They state procedures for handling problems before they arise.

(4) They become an instrument of peace. Misunderstandings and ill feelings are saved in the solving of disagreements.

(5) They place responsibility of action where it belongs—on the people who made the rules and not on those who are responsible for enforcing them.

A constitution and bylaws should be kept up to date by revisions and amendments. Members need to learn that their constitution and bylaws are the instrument by which they govern themselves.

2. *Parliamentary Rules*

F. H. Kerfoot in his book *Parliamentary Law* defines parliamentary law as "that system of rules by which deliberative assemblies govern themselves." He maintains that in the absence of these rules "each individual will act according to his own inclination; no one will know what his rights are, nor how he is to proceed; and in such assemblies, if any business is transacted at all, it will be done amid confusion and disorder, and will likely be controlled by the shrewdest or the loudest."

A system of parliamentary rules is especially needed in Baptist meetings because of their congregational form of government. Sometimes democracy becomes "mobocracy" without these rules. In fact, it was his failure to keep order in the business meeting of a Baptist church that led Henry Robert to prepare and publish what has become America's most famous handbook on parliamentary procedure,

Robert's Rules of Order. First published in 1876, it is widely acclaimed as the nation's bible of parliamentary procedure.

Parliamentary rules are needed primarily to safeguard the rights and privileges of all members. These rules insure that the business meetings will be conducted in an orderly, uniform, and deliberate manner. By applying them, a congregation can make decisions without confusion and delay.

Each church and denominational body should carefully determine a sound system of parliamentary rules in keeping with its particular needs and desires. It is advisable that one of the published handbooks be adopted as the foundation of the system and then any change or adaption of the rules be incorporated in the bylaws of the constitution.

3. *Church Council*

A church council is not a legislative or an executive body. It has no authority. It exercises no controls over the organizations or their activities. It makes no decisions except to recommend to the church for its action. Its work is representative and advisory.

Although the church council is not a governing body, it is a necessary and valuable instrument of government. It contributes to the effectiveness of the governmental processes. It helps to maintain democracy within a church.

The composition of the church council harmonizes with the democratic ideal. It is usually composed of the pastor, staff leaders, chairman of deacons, and organizational heads. Often committee chairmen whose work is related to the work of the council are invited to attend. The council should be large enough to be representative but not too large to be efficient. Usually the pastor will be the chairman and a secretary will be selected by members of the group.

J. M. Crowe lists the following purposes of a church council:

1. It should develop long-range and short-term objectives and goals for the church as a whole and for its organizations. . . .

2. It should outline a church calendar of activities for accomplishing these objectives and goals. . . .

3. It should develop hearty co-operation between all organizations. . . . .

4. It should evaluate results.[3]

As a church council seeks to accomplish these purposes, it draws the organization and the church together in a close working relationship. A real sense of teamwork is developed. The larger purposes of the church become the concern of all members. They work together to correlate their programs.

In the council meetings, problems are faced and solutions determined. Needs are presented and provisions are suggested. Duplications and overlappings are eliminated. Conflicts and their accompanying tensions are avoided. Divisive influences are prevented. Harmony is achieved in the relationships between organizational leaders.

IV. Decisions Reached Through Democratic Action

The basic requirement of church government based on congregational polity is that decisions be reached through democratic action. This is accomplished by well-attended business meetings, thorough discussion of motions, and serious consideration given to voting.

1. Business Meetings Well Attended

One of the weakest points in Southern Baptist government has developed in recent years—the disinclination of

---

[3] "The Church Council Meets a Need," *Church Administration,* I (October, 1959), 9.

church members to attend the business meetings of their churches. Perhaps the cut-and-dried manner of reaching decisions has contributed to this situation. Nevertheless, the poorest attended meetings of many congregations is the regular business meeting. One church of several thousand members requires only a quorum of one hundred present to conduct its business. Only a small fraction of the membership makes the decisions of a supposedly pure democracy.

Business meetings should be democratic with information of items to come before the church distributed in advance. In congregational and organizational meetings a strong emphasis and appeal could be made for acceptance of personal responsibility in congregational government. Personal and written invitations could also be used with profit.

Messengers also need to be enlisted to attend the annual conventions. A common practice is for churches to wait until just before these meetings and then vote that the pastor and his wife and any others who can attend be the messengers. A church should be just as selective and diligent in securing messengers for annual denominational meetings as it is in securing workers to serve in the organizations.

2. Motions Thoroughly Discussed

A pastor accepted the call to another field of service. During his ministry with the church he had led the members to see the merits of the rotation plan for deacons and the congregation adopted it. A few of the older men never became reconciled to the new plan, however. In the first business meeting after the pastor had moved, one of these men was the moderator. Another made the motion that the rotation system be abolished and that all deacons in the church be declared active. Still another quickly seconded the motion and the moderator just as quickly put it to vote. The members, hardly aware of what was going on, perfunctorily raised their hands in approval.

This was not democracy in action. It was more a case of democratic inaction. Afterwards, many who had voted in favor of the motion regretted doing so.

In order for decisions to be reached through democratic action, opportunity for free and adequate discussion must be provided. Both sides of a question should be presented and debated if necessary. All persons have the right to express themselves and should be encouraged to do so. If they do not do so openly in public meetings, they will do so in private. This could lead to dissension and factions.

A young man registered the complaint that in the adoption of his church's budget the members saw it only a few minutes before the vote was to be taken. He said that there was not even enough time to read it much less make an adequate study of it. Fortunately, some of the members protested the limitation of time and insisted that adoption be delayed until the next Wednesday. This was their right and privilege. The church voted to wait until the next week and at that time were unanimous in adopting the budget. Had the vote been forced through, it is likely that many would have gone away unhappy and would have talked about the undemocratic tactics. It is also unlikely that the church would have been successful in fully subscribing its budget.

Discussion is important in achieving good democratic action. It should be given its rightful place in arriving at decisions.

3. *Voting Taken Seriously*

The following notice appeared in the Sunday bulletin of a church:

CHURCH TO DECIDE ON CHURCH
FURNITURE WEDNESDAY

In the vestibule this morning you will
find samples of church furniture. Each
sample is numbered. Please examine
these samples today or sometime before next Wednesday.

Come to the business meeting prepared to vote on the furniture for our
auditorium. We will vote by the num-
bers on the samples so be sure to notice
the number of your choice.

How many churches would have taken the matter of
selecting furniture seriously enough to call for congregational selection and action? Most would have left it to a
small committee and denied the people the joy of helping
to decide on the furnishings of their church.

The seriousness of voting may be emphasized by the
manner in which the vote is taken. Matters which are presented periodically to the church, such as the regular
monthly reports or the election of a worker to fill a vacancy, may be voted by voice or the raising of hands.
A standing vote may be asked for on such important matters as adopting a budget or entering a building program.
The secret ballot could be required for such things as calling a pastor or changing the constitution.

Requiring an interval of time between the making of a
motion and the taking of the vote also emphasizes the seriousness of voting. When major decisions are involved, this
practice allows time for members to consider the facts and
to seek the leadership of the Lord. For example, one
church has in its constitution that it may be changed or
amended only after a waiting period of sixty days and the
bylaws after a period of thirty days.

This keeps a few who may be present in a business meeting from making changes in the church's constitutional government without notice being given to all members that such action is pending. Such a provision prevents action from being taken under such circumstances. It also brings into focus the importance of voting intelligently and prayerfully.

Voting in a church or convention should always be considered a grave responsibility. Each vote cast should be an expression of what an individual considers to be the will of God. Therefore, voting should be preceded by careful consideration and earnest prayer. It is one of the most serious responsibilities that the Christian has in his church.

W. C. Fields has sounded an important note concerning our Baptist democracy.

Democracy in action often requires patience, and generally it is time-consuming, but more often than not wisdom generally prevails. . . . Since verbal inspiration is such a rare quality with us mortals, this majority opinion is still one of the greatest bulwarks of our Baptist life.

Those who truly seek the good of all will gladly submit their ideas to proper appraisal. When we can do this, and then happily abide by the judgments of democratic action, then and only then do we deserve the name of New Testament Christianity.[4]

---

[4] *The Baptist Program* (October, 1960), p. 39.

Suggestions for the Teacher

CHAPTER 1

Prior to the first session ask three class members to report on the government of the Congregationalists, the Adventists, and the Disciples of Christ.

Lead the class to discuss differing views concerning the church universal, and to summarize what Baptists believe.

CHAPTER 2

Divide the class into two groups and let them take opposing views on the statement: "New Testament principles of polity may be adapted, changed, or added to according to the demands of a changing society." After a brief period, let the chosen recorders present the arguments of their respective groups.

CHAPTER 3

List on the chalkboard the four subheads under "The Responsibilities of Members in a Church." Ask the class to give examples of how these principles can be practiced.

CHAPTER 4

Enlist three persons to serve on a panel to discuss church discipline. Have them read and comment on the following Scripture passages: Matthew 18:15-17; Romans 16:17; and 1 Corinthians 5:9-13.

Ask the class to direct their questions to the panel.

CHAPTER 5

Secure for distribution the pamphlets "The Executive Committee of the Southern Baptist Convention," Executive Committee, SBC, Office of Public Relations, 460 James Robertson Parkway, Nashville, Tennessee 37219; and "Get Acquainted with Southern Baptists," Baptist state conventions.

Before discussing this chapter, distribute copies of pamphlets to class members and ask them to read and make notations of statements they want clarified.

Be prepared to answer questions on material in pamphlets.

CHAPTER 6

Write on the chalkboard: Are people ever justified in rejecting civil laws? Ask the class to look at the statement on page 79: "Only when the laws of state are in opposition to the laws of God are Christians justified in rejecting them."

In leading the discussion, use examples of groups such as conscientious objectors, members of sects who refuse blood transfusions, snake handlers, and adherents of passive resistance who claim that their actions are motivated by allegiance to divine law.

CHAPTER 7

Lead class members to give examples of practices that fall under the nine drifts mentioned in this chapter. This can be done after the discussion of each drift or at the conclusion of the teaching period.

CHAPTER 8

Distribute to the class mimeographed copies of your church's constitution and bylaws. Ask members to comment on the value of this document. Have them discuss who is responsible for amendments and revisions.

If your church does not have a constitution and bylaws, ask members to discuss the need for them.

Enlist a church council member to discuss his role in planning, co-ordinating, and evaluating the church program.

For Review and Written Work

CHAPTER 1

1. What is meant by "polity"?
2. How does government differ from polity?
3. Why is there a need for government in a church?
4. Name the four general types of church polity found in the churches of the United States.

CHAPTER 2

5. Why do Baptists base their polity on the Bible?
6. What three concepts of polity grow out of the idea of the triune God?
7. Why is it necessary to democratic processes that the church have a regenerated membership?
8. Give three biblical illustrations of voluntary church co-operation.

CHAPTER 3

9. Why do Baptists believe each individual is of supreme value?
10. How can members of unequal abilities and background be equal in a Baptist church?
11. List the responsibilities of a church member.

CHAPTER 4

12. Why do Baptists reject the idea of a super Church?
13. What is the only basis for true unity in a church?
14. What are the ties that bind Baptists together in their work as a denomination?
15. List major matters which are to be decided by the congregation in business session.

CHAPTER 5

16. What wrong ideas are conveyed by the designation "Southern Baptist Convention church"?
17. List the three denominational bodies.

18. Why is the term "messenger" used instead of "delegate" to identify the individuals who make up a denominational body?

CHAPTER 6

19. Give three reasons why religious liberty is a basic principle in Baptist belief.

20. In what areas of its work does the state recognize the church as a spiritual entity?

21. At what point does the church's business come under the jurisdiction of the state?

CHAPTER 7

22. How can Baptists drift into ritualism in their church government?

23. What is the danger involved in the drift toward officialism?

24. What is the logical outcome if all these drifts are allowed to continue?

CHAPTER 8

25. How can church and denominational leaders help maintain a true democracy?

26. Mention three safeguards for democratic control.

27. How can the manner in which a vote is taken give emphasis to the seriousness of the matter under consideration?

Glossary

Authoritarianism—The surrender of individual freedom of judgment and action to the power and influence of those in leadership positions.

Autocracy—Supreme government by an individual.

Autonomy—Self-government without outside control.

Baptist body—A church, an association, a state convention, or the Southern Baptist Convention.

Bylaws—The secondary rules which make effective the principles and regulations set forth in a constitution.

Centralism—The transfer of governmental functions from the people to the administrators.

Coercion—The act of compelling or restraining by force.

Congregational polity—The form of government in which supreme authority is vested in the congregation.

Constitution—A written statement setting forth the basic principles and regulations by which a group governs itself.

Democracy—Government in which the supreme power is retained by the people and exercised either directly or indirectly.

Denominational body—An association, a state convention, or the Southern Baptist Convention.

Denominationalism—Devotion to denominational principles or interests.

Diocese—The district in which a bishop has authority.

Drift—Movement, either consciously or subconsciously, toward a place, object, effect, or result.

Ecclesiasticism—The recognition of the super Church made up of local churches with ascending levels of authority.

Episcopal polity—The form of government in which bishops oversee the affairs of churches.

Expediency—Subordination of principles for the sake of facilitating an end or purpose.

Federalism—The habit of otherwise autonomous bodies subordinating their authority in affairs common to all to a higher authority.

Government—The implementation and application of polity.

Hierarchy—A body of rulers classified by ranks and orders, with each subordinate to the one above it.

Liberalism—The belief that polity should be fluid and easily adapted to changing needs and to new situations.

Messenger—An elected representative of a church to the annual meetings of the association, the state convention, or the Southern Baptist Convention.

Monarchial polity—The form of government in which authority is centered in one supreme head.

Officialism—The strict adherence to the methods, procedures, plans, and requirements which church or denominational leaders promote and with which they are identified.

Oligarchy—Government in which the ruling powers belong to a few.

Order—Any of the grades or ranks of the ministry in denominations practicing episcopal or monarchial polity.

Organization—The formal arrangement or pattern wherby church members relate themselves to one another for accomplishing the tasks of a church.

Polity—The theory and the framework of government.

Presbyterian polity—The form of government in which authority is vested in presbyters, or elders, on ascending levels.

Program—Any basic continuing activity which has primary importance in achieving church objectives.

Protectionism—The suppression of criticism and information under the guise of the strong protecting the weak; the informed, the ignorant; and the sophisticated, the innocent.

Religious liberty—The freedom of choice and the freedom from compulsion in all matters pertaining to one's religious beliefs, practices, and observances.

Ritualism—The practice of rigidly following procedures and perfunctorily going through the motions of an activity.

Soul-competency—The belief that regenerated man is capable of self-determination and should be left free to act from inner compulsion.

Theocracy—Government by the immediate direction of God.

Traditionalism—Equating traditional ways of doing things with doctrines.

Unanimity—State or quality of being of one mind.